Praise for *Whole Body Intelligence*

"My customers are some of the toughest around: the FBI, US Marshals, and the US Defense Department. Since becoming whole body intelligent, ideas come easier, answers come quicker, and I am told I exude a quiet confidence. Do yourself a favor—read this book and take some action. You, too, will be better off for it."

—DAVID HALE, CEO, DHA Group, Inc.

"This is the intelligence everyone needs! Whole Body Intelligence *will help you navigate life more easily. It helps me understand unconscious messages my body cues tell me and transforms negative beliefs I carried into positive ones all by using the intelligence of my own body."*

—RACHAEL O'MEARA, sales manager, Google

"Steve granted me a huge gift by helping me reclaim my relationship with my body so I can learn to feel and interpret what my body is telling me. It has become a tuning fork that guides me in all aspects of my life. My work with Steve has helped me reclaim my health, heal unhealthy relationship patterns, grow on my spiritual path, and heal my money issues so I can rewrite the script of the movie of my life."

—LISSA RANKIN, MD,
New York Times **bestselling author of** *Mind Over Medicine*

"As someone dedicated to mastering the art of living and moving in the body, Steve Sisgold offers practical tools for enhancing all aspects of my life. Everyone can benefit from Steve's brilliance!"

—DEBBIE ROSAS,
cocreator and founder, Nia, and coauthor of *The Nia Technique*

WHOLE
BODY
INTELLIGENCE

WHOLE BODY

INTELLIGENCE

Get Out of Your Head and Into
Your Body to Achieve Greater Wisdom,
Confidence, and Success

STEVE SISGOLD

Foreword by Lissa Rankin, MD

RODALE.

© 2015 by Steve Sisgold

Rodale books may be purchased for business or promotional use
or for special sales. For information, please write to:
Special Markets Department, Rodale Inc.,
733 Third Avenue, New York, NY 10017

Printed in the United States of America
Rodale Inc. makes every effort to use acid-free ∞, recycled paper ♲.

Book design by Carol Angstadt

Library of Congress Cataloging-in-Publication Data is on file with the publisher.

ISBN 978–1–62336–617–9   trade hardcover

Distributed to the trade by Macmillan

2 4 6 8 10 9 7 5 3 1   hardcover

We inspire and enable people to improve their lives and the world around them.
rodalebooks.com

To my beloveds, who took every step of this ride with me.

Amanda, your unwavering love, support, and wise soul inspire me to live a life of infinite possibilities.

Champ, you sat next to me during the writing of every page of this book and created a feeling of comfort and ease for which I am so grateful. Even though you crossed over the rainbow bridge before its launch, your stories and spirit will live on forever in these pages.

CONTENTS

FOREWORD BY LISSA RANKIN, MD   xi

ACKNOWLEDGMENTS   xv

INTRODUCTION: LET'S TALK STORY   xix

PART I
BEGIN THE JOURNEY

CHAPTER 1—**BODY FIRST: EVERY MOMENT
IS A CHOICE POINT**   3

CHAPTER 2—**THE MAKING OF WHOLE BODY INTELLIGENCE**   19

CHAPTER 3—**HOW DO YOU MOVE THROUGH LIFE?**   51

CHAPTER 4—**YOUR MOVEMENT AUTOBIOGRAPHY**   67

PART II
DESTRESS ON DEMAND

CHAPTER 5—**STRESS: IT'S NOT ALL IN YOUR HEAD**   93

CHAPTER 6—**THE REBOOTING TECHNIQUE**   121

PART III
TRANSFORM LIMITING BELIEFS

CHAPTER 7—**THE ISSUES ARE IN YOUR TISSUES**   147

CHAPTER 8—**IDENTIFYING AND CHANGING VIRAL BELIEFS
INTO VITAL ONES**   171

PART IV
CREATE POSITIVE CHANGES
THAT LAST

CHAPTER 9—**THE WBI 30-DAY LIFESTYLE PLAN**   197

CHAPTER 10—**STAY ENGAGED AND PURPOSEFUL—
NO MATTER WHAT!**   237

CONCLUSION—YOU ARE THE LOTTERY   261
RESOURCES FOR STAYING WHOLE BODY INTELLIGENT   265
INDEX   269

FOREWORD

AS CHILDREN, WE OFTEN get programmed with limiting, self-sabotaging beliefs by our parents. Unbeknownst to them, our well-intentioned mothers and fathers were programmed with limiting, self-sabotaging beliefs themselves and passed them along to us. We are not conscious of most of these limiting beliefs. They live in our subconscious mind, where they create our reality like a thwarted computer operating system.

I firmly believe that if life is a movie, we are the scriptwriters and movie directors of the story of our lives. We are not victims of random, haphazard, traumatizing events inflicted upon us by a hostile Universe. Instead, we are cocreating reality with a Divine force, and the script of what we are cocreating is often written into the subconscious mind from programs we inherited from painful moments in childhood.

For example, a self-sabotaging belief like "Good people are not wealthy, and wealthy people are not good" would play out as money challenges in the movie of your life. A belief that says "All good things come from struggle" requires you to work very hard for any blessings and can block effortlessness and ease. A belief that Mommy abandoned you because you are unlovable might create a movie full of dysfunctional relationships and abandonment issues. Reality is always trying to create coherence between your unconscious beliefs and the events of your life. So if your unconscious belief is that you have to be in poverty to be a good person, you will find ways to ensure that you are financially struggling, because your desire to be a good person will override your conscious desire to acquire wealth.

But here's the good news. You are not a helpless victim of your life. You can heal your limiting beliefs and rewrite your movie script, and Steve Sisgold is here to help you learn how. I don't give this endorsement lightly—it comes from personal experience because Steve is my therapist, and I trust what he teaches. I have done Whole Body Intelligence sessions that have helped me uncover what Steve calls "viral beliefs," hidden like viruses in the body, and have showed me how to release them and embody new "vital beliefs."

My work with Steve has been absolutely, unequivocally life-changing. After 12 years of medical education, I had become a walking cerebrum, completely dissociated from the compass of my body. After all, as a doctor, I couldn't sleep when I was tired, eat when I was hungry, or go to the bathroom when I was scrubbed into the operating room. I had to come to work when my body was sick. And I wound up taking seven prescription medications by the time I was 33. My body was literally screaming at me, but I had learned to dissociate from it in order to survive the almost inhuman levels of physical and emotional trauma that accompany medical education.

Steve granted me a huge gift by helping me reclaim my relationship with my body so I could learn to feel and interpret what my body was telling me. It has become a tuning fork that guides me in all aspects of my life. My body compass guides me as part of my spiritual guidance, right alongside my intuition and external "signs from the Universe," which often appear as almost miraculous synchronicities. I have learned how to use sensations in my body as a marker of limiting beliefs that get stuck in my body, beliefs which must be healed before I can write joyful, effortless success, health, love, and miracles into the movie of my life. I have learned how to clear these beliefs in my body through the kinds of techniques you will learn in this book.

Because limiting beliefs can be such blind spots from the conscious mind, most of us aren't even aware of the viral beliefs that run our lives. They operate as unconscious programs without any awareness in the conscious mind. Yet, as our collective consciousness begins to wake up, more and more of us are becoming aware of these limiting beliefs that hold us back from living smack dab in the center of our purpose. As these beliefs come into awareness, those of us brave enough to do deep psychological and spiritual work need the kinds of tools taught in this book in order to free ourselves from whatever weighs us down and holds us back from our capacity to create miracles in our lives and on the planet.

My work with Steve has helped me reclaim my health, heal unhealthy relationship patterns, grow on my spiritual path, and heal my money issues so I can rewrite the script of the movie of my life. This is still an ongoing process for me.

I suspect you may also have limiting beliefs like I do, beliefs that are holding you back from stepping fully and vibrantly into your richest, most loving, meaningful, passionate, fulfilling life. Rachel Naomi Remen said, "You can't force a rosebud to blossom by beating it with a hammer," and I know this is true. None of us can be forced into awakening. But this book can be your fertilizer. As Anaïs Nin said, "And the day came when the risk to remain tight in a bud was more painful than the risk it took to blossom." Let this book help you burst into full bloom with all the aliveness in your beautiful, trustworthy heart.

—LISSA RANKIN, MD,
New York Times bestselling author
of *Mind Over Medicine*

ACKNOWLEDGMENTS

IT TAKES A VILLAGE. When I took some deep breaths to tune in to the people I wanted to highlight in this section, I first saw in my mind's eye those of you who stood opposite me during a WBI session or sat in a circle at a workshop or a retreat. Most of all, it is all of you who helped me develop and refine my program, my life, and this book. A huge mahalo goes out to every one of you.

I give gratitude to the many radio, TV, and webinar hosts who asked me thought-provoking questions and provided brilliant insights into the body of work that was crystallized into this book.

To my good friend and literary agent Michele Martin. Thank you for believing in me and immersing yourself personally into WBI. Your edits and ideas were genius and kept stretching me to bring out the most authentic, revealing book that resided within me. I am also very grateful for the other members of my super bowl agent team, Steve and Gabriel Harris. You nailed it and carried me through every stage of the process. I am blessed to have you three watching my back.

To my dream publisher, Rodale. You have been trailblazing wellness and healthy living for millions through your magazines and books, and I am honored to be part of your family and mission. To my editor, Ursula Cary Ziemba, your genuine enthusiasm and commitment to excellence for *Whole Body Intelligence* deserves a standing ovation. Your talent and your innate instincts coupled with your ability to care for your author and his audience have made this journey very special, enlightening, and exciting for me. I also bow with respect to the other members of the Rodale team who embraced this project with brilliance, creativity, and special care, including Jess Fromm, Hope Clarke, Paula Brisco, Carol Angstadt, Jeff Batzli, Emily Eagan, and Brent Gallenberger.

Lissa Rankin, I am imagining that I am handing you a gorgeous Hawaiian lei of pink, white, and yellow plumerias, as I am chanting a huge mahalo to you for writing the foreword to this book and so much more. My appreciation for having you in my life is limitless, just like you are. I love that we share the same birthday and celebrate holidays and call each other family. That is an honor I hold and cherish dearly. I have met many authors and thought leaders in my field of work, but none as generous, transparent, and loving as you.

A big round of applause goes to my writing guru, teacher, editor extraordinaire, and special friend Geralyn Gendreau. More than anyone, you have taught me over the past 6 years the art of communicating on the written page. The way you show me how to get my points and stories across in a succinct yet compelling way is invaluable. Like I have said to you many times, "Often when I am writing, I sense you over my shoulder; then the perfect words flow through." From the deepest source of my soul, I am beyond grateful for our alliance and relationship.

And I send out a very special thanks to Anila, for being the person I send my final drafts to before submitting my chapters. It always amazes me how your attention to detail and ability to keep me on track is so valuable and always right on.

Infinite thanks to Gay Hendricks, Kathlyn Hendricks, Jocelyn Olivier, Dr. Kay Corpus, and Christine Landon, for your generous time and wisdom that you shared in our interviews.

I praise Ernie Hubbard for your dedication and genius in conducting the study and providing innovative ideas and spectacular data and visuals to demonstrate the rebooting technique's effectiveness.

Big recognition goes to the devoted team at Preventive Medical Center of Marin, for including me as a member of your top-shelf medical team and integrative practice. I especially want to thank Dr. Elson Haas, Dr. Richard Shames, Dr. Michael Rosenberg, and Julie Dietz for your many referrals and unwavering belief in WBI.

A special shout-out goes to my spirit/mastermind team— Lissa Rankin, Amy Ahlers, Christine Arylo, and Mike Robbins— who dove deep, spoke truth, and held me in my highest visions. Just looking at your names here and realizing what an amazing team I manifested is one of the true blessings of doing this work so I can meet and collaborate with people like you.

To my long time buddy and Scrabble opponent Steve Keyser, I thank you for your devoted friendship, authentic interest in my book, and the very generous promotion and publicity services you graciously offer without me even asking.

To my longest lifetime friend since the second grade, Ted Levenson. I am blessed by your constant affirmations reminding me that I "actualize and am a winner!" Those two vital messages you consistently give me are embedded in my core;

because of you, I carry them with me through the many mazes of life.

To Steve Bond and Pamela Blount, thank you dearly for stepping up as not only cousins but as real-life angels to my mom, which has provided me with comfort and a special kind of love in my heart, while writing this book.

To my family. Tillye Sisgold, you were my biggest cheerleader in life, and I was fortunate to have had you in that role from day one and throughout the process of writing this book. In your recent transition to be with Dad, I want you to know I miss you every day. When I think of you, I know how blessed I was to have had such positive reinforcement and how that is a big part of why I am who I am today.

Jesse Sisgold, my main, main man. Who you are is way beyond anything I could have dreamed up. You are my best friend, the most caring son, and the funniest person I know. I observe you and how you move through and interact with life, and it sets bars for me to reach in the years I have left here on earth. Speaking of gifts, I am so fortunate to have the best daughter in law imaginable, Kristina Brittenham. Your love of our family is a blessing, and your "I am so proud of you D" texts and e-mails light me up more than you know. You are also an amazing mom, which is the reason I get to thank the light of my life last but not least, Eleanor Marin Sisgold.

My favorite dialogue in life is when I ask "How much does G PA love Eleanor?" and you answer on cue "All the way." Since you came into my life, my happiness quotient has risen beyond measure. When I am with you, I get to experience true freedom in my whole body. Thank you for that invaluable gift.

INTRODUCTION

LET'S TALK STORY

WITH ITS VIEW OF craters and mountains in the distance, Keawakapu is one of the most spectacular beaches on the south side of Maui. Among native Hawaiians, Keawakapu is also a focal point for ceremonies and prayer. Its rich history and spectacular sunsets make it the perfect setting to hold the last day of my weeklong Whole Body Intelligence (WBI) trainings. To help me give a proper Hawaiian-style send-off to participants, I always invite my friend Puanani Mahoe, a kahuna known as Auntie Pua, to lead a portion of our closing ceremonies. In Hawaii the kahuna are an important part of the culture. Through time they served the king and queen and assisted the people in practical ways as healers, builders, navigators, and philosophers. A modern-day Hawaiian kahuna functions primarily as a priest and shaman who ministers to the people. I was excited for the group to see the way Pua "talks story" through her chants, her body movements, and her singsong words; all in such a congruent, effortless whole-body-intelligent way.

Auntie Pua stood facing the ocean as we watched the full palette of sunset blaze across the sky. She wore a ceremonial headdress made of flowers, leaves, and shells. Her regal bearing caused all of those gathered to fall silent. I watched as she raised her arm, brought a conch shell to her mouth, and broke the silence with a deep, hollow drone. Auntie Pua blew her *pu*—the Hawaiian word for conch shell—to say good-bye to the day and express her gratitude with the sound. Once she'd performed this simple blessing, she bowed and said, "Mahalo."

We stood watching with tangible awe. Many of us had come from far away and had never stood on a white sand beach like this. For several in the group, it was the first time they heard the sound of a conch shell. Everyone was breathing in and out deeply and enjoying a whole-body experience, from head to toe.

I first met Auntie Pua when she officiated a friend's wedding on Makena Beach. After the wedding party, she invited me to walk with her down the beach. We strolled along the brilliant white sand, flanked by black lava rock on one side and the blue-green ocean on the other. She asked me to join her in *kukakuka,* saying, "You've heard the pidgin (slang) term 'talk story,' yes?" She went on to explain, "*Kukakuka* is how we get to know ourselves and each other better." I nodded my consent as she spread a brightly colored sarong on the sand. Auntie Pua began our *kukakuka* session with an invitation. She requested that I shift my attention away from my everyday cares and concerns and fully engage in the moment with her, as we talk story. Pua was asking me to be present with her in my mind and body.

The Hawaiian people know what cultures throughout time have known: that when we naturally connect with ourselves, we connect better with others and can truly share practical wisdom and insights. We can keep family memories alive, explore cultural patterns, share and decipher our dreams. Stories are also a marvelous aid to help us reflect on autobiographical events that have influenced the way we live and view the world today.

Intrigued by my conversation with Pua, I started having childhood flashbacks. I was sitting on the front porch of my childhood home in a row-house neighborhood north of Baltimore. I could hear my cousins giggling as we all sat around while our parents, grandparents, uncles, and aunts talked story. I heard the elders telling tales about the old country, their travels and migrations from Poland and Russia, and setting up shop in America. I recalled some of my relatives' stories about growing up in the inner-city streets of Baltimore. I remember the laughter, the hilarity, and the tears. Those hours on the porch were highly entertaining. They also contributed to my sense of self and of my place in the world. To this day I love how I feel when I retell some of those stories in speeches and writing and at the dinner table with friends.

Talking story is one of many ways that a person's self-concept is forged. Talking story offers us an opportunity to objectively look at family traits and behaviors we absorbed, and high-impact moments that influenced attitudes and beliefs we developed, that might be getting in our way today.

I invite you to talk story with me in the pages that follow. I'm making the same invitation to you that Auntie Pua extended to me: to engage fully; to give yourself the time and the willingness to shift your attention and stay present with your body, your emotions, and your mind as you read. In this book there will be many opportunities for you to talk story between your mind and body through specific exercises designed to give you access to your *whole* body's intelligence. Take full advantage of using this expanded perspective to glimpse what you otherwise might not be able to see. Once you've gotten that first glimpse, you will begin to recognize patterns and imprints that have lived beneath your everyday awareness. Throughout the book I will guide and encourage you to uncover the roots of those unconscious patterns that live in your body and help you change them. My personal stories and those of clients who did this work will remind you that you are not alone.

The book you have in your hands, *Whole Body Intelligence,* will provide you with a trusty skill set and a new awareness that consistently keep you in touch with your inner navigator—your personal Google, if you will. It will show you that your body is always ready to give you the most reliable information, indicate the best way to go, and reveal the best decision to make. You'll feel more relaxed, knowing that you can make difficult decisions without strenuous mental gymnastics. No more overthinking. No more lying awake at night strategizing your next best move—just you trusting what you know and acting with confidence.

Whole Body Intelligence will show you how to get out of

your head and use essential body-centered life skills to take charge of every area of your life with increased awareness, clarity, and confidence. Many self-improvement programs train you to identify and solve problems by thinking them through. This program takes you straight to the body for solutions.

In Chapter 1 you will be introduced to one of the foundational tenets of the WBI approach: *Every moment is a choice point; choose body first.* You will learn how to shift your attention from outer experiences and the thoughts they evoke to the physical response in the body. This will afford you real-time experience of the body-first approach. We'll talk story again and see what happens when you lean into the information from your whole body rather than rely on your thoughts, assumptions, and projections about the matter at hand. Then I will review the science that verifies the body-mind connection.

In Chapter 2, The Making of Whole Body Intelligence, you will get the back story on how this work came to me and developed. I will share how my world transformed when I recognized and then embraced my own innate body-based intelligence. As my passion for WBI grew, I delved deeper into the mind-body field and began to teach others and see the result in thousands of lives.

Initially my curiosity revolved around the question, why are some people more successful than others? I noticed that the most successful people were congruent—their words, attitudes, and body language carried the same message. Meanwhile, people who had less success in their lives were often walking, talking contradictions. Their body language and their words did not line up. These folks were unaware that they were sending mixed messages, that the micromovements in the body told a different story than the words coming out of their mouth. I saw this phenomenon repeated again and again, which led me to study a variety of disciplines. What I learned about breath, movement, awareness, body language, somatic therapy, and cellular memory confirmed my growing sense that the body is a key source of vital information.

By this point you will have gained a better understanding of the importance of the body-first approach and had direct experiences of this valuable resource that can deliver key insights and information when you take the time to tune in.

In Chapter 3, How Do You Move through Life?, you will continue to become more Whole Body Intelligent through advanced self-inquiry. I will lead you through a highly personal exploration of how and why you move the way you do, what your movements communicate to others, and how those subconscious patterns may undermine your greatest desires.

You will explore the power of movement to liberate and change your brain to lessen the power of self-sabotaging patterns rooted in past experiences. You will begin to taste the thrill of moving forward in situations rather than backward and activating a higher-order thinking through your body movements.

In Chapter 4 you will start writing what I call your movement autobiography. Now you will learn, see, and feel how specific movement patterns were formed. Coupled with movement awareness exercises, the movement autobiography can reveal behavioral patterns and knee-jerk reactions that are often carbon copies of what you saw your parents do. Once again we will talk story and hear about individuals who used these exercises to release inner resistance and achieve spectacular results.

In Chapter 5, Stress: It's Not All in Your Head, we tackle the number one silent killer—chronic stress. The endgame is simple: to enable you to destress on demand. We'll look from a number of angles. We'll see why stress-management programs that emphasize cognitive processes are not always effective and instead use the body-first approach to detect, manage, and release stress. We'll even talk about how to reverse its negative effects. I'll ask you to identify specific stressors that are affecting you and investigate the impact they have on your body, your mind, and your emotions.

No chapter on stress would be complete without addressing information overload. I'll present empirical data that verifies what we all intuitively know: Technology carries a heavy payload of stress on your body. I will talk about the fallacy of multitasking, which we now know is a major contributor to mental burnout.

In Chapter 6 you will be introduced to another key component of the WBI curriculum: the rebooting technique (TRT). You will learn and practice seven steps to shift stress instantly and experience how TRT helps you redirect your stress response before it steals your life force. You'll learn how TRT can enhance many areas of your life through reports from other physicians, coaches, executives, and therapists who've incorporated the rebooting technique in their personal and professional lives. Individuals and teams use it as a warmup before workouts or athletics, as a method to prepare for a presentation or important social event, as a booster to stay engaged and resilient throughout the day, as well as an immediate intervention tool for anxiety and stress. You will also be given a specific Web link where you can watch me demonstrate the technique on video and where you can print out a PDF of the rebooting steps to have on hand.

I also present the results of a study conducted at the Preventive Medical Center of Marin in San Rafael, California. Patients were taught the rebooting technique while hooked up to diagnostic machines. After doing the steps, stress was reduced an average of 55 percent. Erratic heartbeats became coherent ones.

With the rebooting technique on your tool belt, in Chapters 7 and 8 you will use your whole body's intelligence to identify and change limiting beliefs. In Chapter 7 you learn how your "issues live in your tissues." I provide information from neurological and physiological research to help you understand what limiting beliefs are and explain their tendency to lie dormant not just in the mind but in the body for years, much like physical viruses. We'll discuss traumatic experiences as they relate to negative beliefs that get embedded in the body through physical responses such as holding the breath, freezing up, or going numb to avoid feelings.

By the time you get to Chapter 8, you will be primed to trade in your viral (negative) beliefs for vital (empowering) ones. I'll take you step by step through my process for doing that. Each step is illustrated with client examples and supported by scientific information. And once again you'll receive a Web link to an audio of me demonstrating these steps. You can also download and print a PDF of all the steps to have on hand.

By this point you'll have a strong foundation of WBI and its skill sets—you are ready to go for it, to make positive changes that stick. Chapter 9 shows you exactly how to do that with the WBI 30-Day Lifestyle Plan. All the practices and insights you've gained at this point will converge in this 30-day program designed to retrain your subconscious mind to create lasting change. I provide a series of questions and exercises to bring your WBI lifestyle alive with specific action steps.

The end of our journey together is really the beginning of your personal adventure into the life you truly desire. In Chapter 10 we'll chart the Whole Body Intelligence lifestyle. We'll talk story one last time so you can peer into the lives of people for whom WBI has become their default setting. These inspiring stories will instill in you the conviction and motivation to move forward and integrate this material into every aspect of your life. We'll focus on three key areas you'll want to master so you can maintain a high level of awareness and well-being: how to stay engaged and present in any situation, how to build resilience so you can spring back from challenges and disappointments, and how to embody and express your purpose from head to toe.

As we begin this remarkable adventure into your brilliant body, I'd like to extend you one more invitation. I invite you to be part of the body-first culture that is emerging now that we are collectively realizing the mind alone cannot take us where we want to go. In Hawaii the word for a family is *ohana*, which roughly translates as "a group that breathes together." My invitation to you is to take this journey with me as an ohana, to walk together and breathe together and stay open to re-create our lives in every moment.

Wishing you many blessings on the pathway.

Mahalo,
Steve

PART I

BEGIN THE JOURNEY

CHAPTER 1

BODY FIRST: EVERY MOMENT IS A CHOICE POINT

*It is our choices, Harry, that show us
what we truly are, far more than our abilities.*

—DUMBLEDORE, IN J. K. ROWLINGS'S
HARRY POTTER AND THE CHAMBER OF SECRETS

YOUR ULTIMATE DESTINATION ON this adventure is to fully understand, learn, and practice being Whole Body Intelligent. This chapter is your first stop on the ride. You will practice the skill of shifting your attention from your thinking mind, or what is called mental cognition, to the sensations and information available from your body, i.e., embodied cognition. I call this shift *body first*.

The ability to direct your attention and take a body-first approach is the foundation of Whole Body Intelligence (WBI). Free will is the human ability to make choices that are not determined by external circumstances. We can increase both the reach and effectiveness of our free will when we become keenly aware of where we put our attention.

In the following exercise, you will get your first stamp on your WBI passport through a tangible experience of the body-first approach. To help you feel what I mean, let's go back to Keawakapu Beach, which you visited in the Introduction.

Imagine that you and I are sitting in a couple of comfortable pelican pouch beach chairs. We're watching the ocean waves rise and fall a few feet before us. Hear the waves as they crash on the beach and return to the ocean in a steady rhythm. Smell the salty air, feel the sweet ocean breeze on your skin, see the setting sun spray color across the sky.

Now take a minute and listen to the thoughts passing through your mind. What are they saying? The voice in your head might be comparing the weather in Hawaii to the current temperature where you live. Perhaps you are reflecting on your last vacation or musing about going back to your favorite beach. You may even find that your thoughts free-associate as you start reviewing your bucket list and begin planning that long-overdue scuba-diving trip to Belize. Next thing you know, your mind has wandered off to the other to-dos on your bucket list and you're jumping out of an airplane, living in a village helping kids, or exploring the Mayan ruins. These are typical comments I've heard from clients who came to work with me in Hawaii; these were their responses when I asked, "What are you thinking about as you look at what is in front of you?"

Now that you've witnessed your own thought stream, let's shift your attention.

Go back to the beach scene and engage all of your senses.

See the ocean, hear the wind in the palm trees, feel the warmth of the setting sun. Now intentionally shift your attention from your thoughts to your body.

Take a deep breath in through your nose and exhale through your mouth. Take another deep breath and fill your lungs from bottom to top. Place your hand on your belly; feel your belly expand as you inhale. Release the breath; your exhale will happen with no effort. Now take another deep breath and relax completely.

Continue to place your attention on your breathing and take three more full, deep *belly* breaths in and out. Notice anything you observe that you were not aware of a few moments ago.

Let your body move organically and do whatever it wants. If you are inclined to make a sound on the exhalation or let out a big sigh, do it. If you feel a bit of tension in your neck, follow the urge to roll your head from side to side. Shake your hands to release tension and pent-up energy, if that is your impulse.

Now take one more deep breath in through your nose and allow your jaw to loosen all the way as you exhale. Empty your face of all expression.

Next imagine you are back on the beach. Notice any body sensations that arise. Scan your body from your head to your toes. What do you sense and feel in your body right now?

You just made a fundamental attention shift from a mind-first to a body-first orientation. The focus of your attention went from thinking about the beach scene to experiencing what you feel when you imagine being on that beach. You expanded your experience by engaging with what is happening inside your body in addition to what is going on outside or floating through your mind.

It's important to note that it isn't necessary to silence the mind or stop your thoughts to broaden your attention and include what your body is feeling and telling you. Your mind may frequently wander here and there. If you continue to reorient in this body-first way on a regular basis, however, your thoughts will slow down and allow your body more bandwidth to communicate with you, to give you information, feedback, and direction.

Now that you've had an initial experience of the body-first approach, let's move deeper inside and find out what else your body is telling you.

Again allow your awareness to move inside your skin as you shift your attention away from your thinking mind and attend to the sensations and "felt sense" available when you focus on your body.

Notice what is occurring. You may realize that you are bouncing your knees up and down, tensing your jaw, gripping this book or your tablet tightly.

Next begin a conversation between your body and your mind. For instance, you might say, "I notice butterflies in my belly" or "I seem to be holding tension in my hips, and there's a restless feeling in my legs."

Now shift your attention to some detail outside of you. Perhaps you discover a large stack of papers on your desk. Observe what your body has to say about that pile of papers—you may shake your head a bit or hear a quick "tsk" come out of your mouth.

Go back and forth from your inner experience to how you mentally frame, judge, explain, or make assumptions about what you see.

What have you learned about yourself?

Did certain parts of your body talk to you when you opened your eyes and observed conditions or events outside of your body?

What is your body saying right now?

This is how you begin to have an integrative conversation between your mind and your body.

Keep practicing and noticing what you discover when you include body awareness in your internal dialogue.

When I think about _____, I have the following thoughts:

_____

When I think about _____ and listen to my body, I notice:

_____

Continue and observe any changes in your breathing, posture, body temperature, or body movements.

As you practice this exercise, your body will come alive. No matter what your opinion of your body or your complaints about how your body looks or functions, your body will respond when you shift your attention and listen to what it has to tell you.

THE SECRET TO LIFE: STICK TO ONE THING

In the movie *City Slickers*, 39-year-old Mitch Robbins, played by Billy Crystal, is having a midlife crisis. Robbins's antagonist in the film is the tough-as-nails trail boss, Curly. Midway

ADVANTAGES OF USING
THE BODY-FIRST APPROACH

• Your body readily alerts you when you fall into negative mental traps and conditioned patterns such as assumptions, comparisons, and blame. You instinctively shift your focus and call on your body's intelligence for clarity.

• You are self-aware and alert to subtle body sensations—a tightness in your jaw when not speaking up, the tension in your hand while gripping the phone tightly during a business call, or a twisting feeling in your gut that says "No!" when you are about to make a wrong decision. You know how to access and interpret the meaning of these sensations and link them back to specific life events that negatively influence your behavior.

• Negative thoughts and beliefs that live in your body do not consume or control you. You know how to stop, release, and change them before they sabotage your results.

• You are aware of nonverbal messages you communicate to others. You feel and notice when your words and body language are incongruent, and you self-correct for better results and more authentic communication.

• You detect stress in your body and manage it. You stay engaged, resilient, and present.

• You trust your instincts to inspire you, help you make the best choices, and take decisive action in any situation.

through a grueling cattle drive, Curly gives Mitch some advice about life. He begins by asking Mitch, "Do you know what the secret of life is?"

"No, what?" Mitch replies.

Curly raises his index finger in the air. "This."

"Your finger?" Mitch asks, clueless.

"One thing. Just one thing," Curly answers. "You stick to that and the rest don't mean s!*#."

Unfortunately our minds have a hard time sticking to one thing and often take us on confusing loop-the-loops that generate undesirable circumstances, behaviors, and outcomes. When we take a body-first approach, when we focus on our body as that "one thing" we stick to, we instantly upgrade our perspective and decision-making power in any situation.

You will strengthen and sharpen your body-first skills as you travel through this process. Again and again you will be asked to put your body first and discover what movement and awareness can show you that your mind cannot.

Applying your free will to inhabit your body fully may be a completely foreign experience. For most people it also feels oddly familiar—a place they once knew quite well but forgot about along the way.

OUT OF THE MOUTHS OF BABES

As babies we knew only one orientation to the world—body first. Somatic experience is the primary language of all human beings, regardless of race, culture, country, or native language. Before we started to speak, before we became identified with the thinking mind and our thoughts—with mental cognition—we were utterly dependent on sensation as our source of information. In other words, we relied entirely on embodied cognition. Our skin, our ears, our ability to sense changes in temperature, our vision, our sense of smell and taste, our kinesthetic sense, our ability to process information and transform our experience through movement—all of these are examples of embodied cognition.

I recently witnessed a startling display of this natural ability in my 3-year-old granddaughter, Eleanor.

"Mommy, I have a stomachache," Eleanor complained after coming home from preschool. Apparently there was a stomach virus spreading around.

The next morning her dad came into her room and found her smiling. He asked her, "How are you doing, sweetie? How does your tummy feel?"

Eleanor replied, "I took the tears and pain from my belly and put them in my heart, Dad, and that made it all better."

Eleanor didn't think her way through feeling sick. She was not transfixed by thoughts such as "If I get sick, I'll miss school. What if I'm contagious and make my friends sick?" Rather, she instinctively moved through her feelings and discomfort in her belly at a bodily level. Her belly hurt, so she instinctively moved the pain to her heart so it would feel better and go away. The messages from her body do not get translated into thoughts; she transmuted them in her body in her own way to ease the pain.

HOW WE GET THE MIND TO BUY IN

Before we look at the specifics of how our body intelligence gets usurped by the mind, let's consider the context in which the denial of the body occurs. Understanding the context in which embodied cognition is replaced by mental cognition is important because that context—when grasped by the mind— helps the mind buy in. This buy-in is key for the mind to become predisposed to an alliance with the body. In other words, we'd do well to satisfy the mind's need for mental cognition so it doesn't drag its heels when we cross over into embodied cognition.

That said, here's the context.

René Descartes, the 17th-century philosopher, largely influenced our predominant worldview in Western society. Descartes said, "I think, therefore I am." Cartesian philosophy views the mind and body as dualities, separate and—at times—at odds. Rationality and reason are viewed as superior faculties to be relied on when making decisions. A well-informed mind is seen as the virtuous guide when it comes to our choices and free will.

Whole Body Intelligence and the body-first approach offer you a new definition and experience of free will. To restore the full range of your free will, to return to you what Cartesian philosophy attempted to deny you, we need to catalyze the relationship between your mind and body.

We want to become embodied individuals, to transition out of a disembodied "I think, therefore I am" position to a corporeal alignment: "I think with my body and my mind, therefore I am." This is how you can free yourself from the straitjacket of separation and the adversarial dynamic between you and your body.

A philosophical context alone cannot rob a person of the

brilliance built in the human body. Philosophy can, however, recruit parents, educators—even employers—to impose mind-over-body rule.

Sir Ken Robinson is an English author, speaker, and international advisor in education and the arts. In his 2006 TED talk, Robinson said, "As children grow up, we start to progressively educate them from the waist up." He speaks to the misguided purpose of our current education system—teaching us how to live in our heads, disembodied. He goes on to poke fun at academics who "look upon their body as a form of transport for their heads, a way of getting their heads to meetings."

Child rearing is an equally powerful force in the lives of children. Many of our standard child-rearing practices deny the wisdom of the body and confuse our innate knowing, as the following example shows.

Cucumber Water Is Not Lemonade

Indian Springs is a natural hot springs resort in Calistoga, California. It is one of those places people go to unplug, relax, and enjoy the healing mineral waters. I was enjoying a long, hot soak in the outdoor pool when a motherly voice rippled through the silence: "Honey, you will love this, it's just like lemonade."

My body responded with a tug in the back of my throat that said, "I'm thirsty, I could use a tasty lemonade too," so I opened my eyes.

A woman with her hair wrapped in a bright green towel

was signaling to her toddler, who was happily playing on the pool steps. The woman reached toward the little girl, handing her a plastic cup that looked to me to be filled with the ice water and thin slices of cucumber the resort has by the entrance.

I thought, "Hmmm. I love the cuke water they have at spas, but it definitely does not taste like sweetened lemon juice."

I watched as the little girl took a sip. She scrunched her nose and squirmed a bit as she looked up to her mom. Mom's disappointment was instant and tangible; her face fell and her body visibly collapsed—shoulders and all.

I felt empathy for the mom; she so wanted her daughter to like the green water. But comparing it to lemonade?

I felt even more empathy for the daughter. She knew how the drink tasted to her, and it wasn't at all like lemonade.

The mother's agenda was fairly obvious: "You need to agree with me and enjoy this like I do, or I will be disappointed." For a young child (or even an adult), disappointing a parent or failing to meet their expectations sets up an internal conflict. If the girl could have put words to her experience, I imagine she would have said, "No, Mommy. It is not yummy, and it doesn't taste like lemonade at all."

But that isn't what I heard. (Okay, I admit it. By this time, I was in full-on eavesdropping mode.)

Mom: "So whatcha think? Yummy, huh?"

Daughter, with head down: "It's okay."

Mom: "Just okay? I think it's yummy. I love it. How can you not like it? You will. Try it again. Give it another try."

Daughter blinked her eyes several times, then looked right

at Mom: "I'll try it again. I'll think of it as green lemonade."
She took another drink and forced a smile. So did her mom.

What Really Happened?

The little girl gave up her body's authority in favor of Mom's
authority. Mother's certainty and need for her daughter to
agree caused the little girl to override her body-based knowledge. She drank more and pretended she liked it to please her
mom, not her palate.

This may seem like a harmless interaction, yet this type of
undue influence over children's built-in, body-based intelligence conditions them to ignore and even distrust what their
body is telling them.

Once we become far removed from our bodily experience,
it becomes easy to ignore any physical or emotional signals
that don't fit into our mental constructs. This becomes a
habit—our default response to the world. When we repeatedly
and persistently respond to the world through disembodied
constructs, we move further away from WDI. And all this happens without our knowing it. We form these habits of mind
unconsciously, and then we reinforce them with technology's
many "smart" devices that make it even easier to ignore our
body in favor of a nonstop data stream.

On the other hand, we need not go farther than your bathroom sink to see your body's brilliance in action. From opening the cap on a tube of toothpaste to dragging a sharp razor
down your cheek or leg, your body performs a remarkable

array of tasks without the least bit of fuss. We call these *habits*, routine patterns your body takes you through as a matter of course. What's interesting about this from a body-first perspective is that we can't change a habit if we rely solely on the mind.

In *Breaking the Habit of Being Yourself*, Joe Dispenza, DC, explains:

> What most people don't know is that when they think about a highly charged emotional experience, they make the brain fire in the exact sequences and patterns as before; they are firing and wiring their brains to the past by reinforcing those circuits into ever more hardwired networks. They also duplicate the same chemicals in the brain and body (in varying degrees) as if they were experiencing the event again in that moment. Those chemicals begin to train the body to further memorize that emotion. Both the chemical results of thinking and feeling, feeling and thinking, as well as the neurons firing and wiring together, condition the mind and the body into a finite set of automatic programs.
>
> We are capable of reliving a past event over and over, perhaps thousands of times in one lifetime. It is this unconscious repetition that trains the body to remember that emotional state, equal to or better than the conscious mind does. When the body remembers better than the conscious mind—that is, when the body *is* the mind—that's called a *habit*.

Let's take a look at a highly charged emotional experience and see how these habits of mind might play out.

HABITS OF MIND IN ACTION

Imagine you have been wrapping up the final details on a monster project at work. You've just finished a 2-hour meeting with your team; you walk out of the conference room and head toward your office. You feel a sense of relief and elation that you have finally cleared the deck so you can leave work behind. Tomorrow morning you are leaving town with the family for a 2-week vacation in Europe.

You round the corner and see your desk. There is a pile of papers sitting right in front of your keyboard. Atop the stack is a note from your boss saying he needs these reports completed by Wednesday noon.

You immediately begin to verbalize your frustration: "This isn't happening. He's not serious." You slam the file you're carrying on the desk and start an internal rant: "What part of 'on vacation' don't you understand? I exceeded all your performance markers this year. *This cannot be happening!*"

Your mind races to your family, to your son who has been reading travel guides aloud at the dinner table for weeks. "It will take me the better part of 5 days to get this done!"

Then you notice the familiar sound and feel of your inner tirade. You identify your experience as the knee-jerk reaction we've been talking about: You've gone into your head and let your automatic thoughts take over. In a split-second moment of clarity, you realize that if you continue down this road, your automatic habits of mind, and the behaviors that accompany them, will soon take over.

Instead you pause and remind yourself that you do have a

choice. You choose to put your body first and tune in.

You take a few deep breaths, scan your body, and notice that you are extremely tense—about an 8 on a scale of 1 to 10.

Without this shift in focus, you would already be entangled in your mind-first reaction, unaware of the tension in your body. If you allowed the angry thoughts to escalate, you might hold your breath or start to hyperventilate, completely unaware that you were doing so. One hundred percent of your attention would be on thoughts about your boss and how rude he is to hand you a large assignment the day before a vacation. You might spend much of the afternoon complaining to your coworkers or worrying how your spouse will react when you tell her or him you have to bring work along on the trip.

Instead you choose to put your body first. You notice what your body is telling you. You feel the angry grip in your hands, the heaviness in your chest, the bottom-out feeling in your gut as you picture getting on the plane, briefcase in hand.

Employing this body-first approach—that is, noticing your emotions and body sensations—gives you the opportunity to take slow, deep breaths; bring yourself into the moment; and establish neutral ground from which to think and feel your way to your next best move. Maintaining this body-aware state, you can take charge and sort out a plan of action. Rather than spinning at your desk for hours, you get proactive. You look over the raw material for the reports and make a list of priority items to present to your boss. You look at the calendar and consider the timing in terms of production and workload for other departments. You review the details, remembering the value of knowing when and what to delegate.

In the end you approach your boss with a clearly outlined plan for getting the time-sensitive reports out on time and a direct request that the balance of the extra work be tabled until you return from vacation.

When you walk into his office, you feel calm and clear-headed. Your body is relaxed. You make your case.

We always have a choice of where we place our attention. We can go into our heads and rely primarily on mental cognition—our thoughts, assumptions, associations, and projections. Or we can turn to our bodies and put our trust in embodied cognition— what the body is telling us in the form of sensations, gut instincts, and feelings.

The aim of this developmental process is to reclaim your native ability to make choices in favor of what you truly desire so you can progress toward your goals. Once your decision-making process is upgraded, you can begin to clarify and align with perhaps the strongest motivator of all: your higher purpose.

As we continue on our journey together in this book, you will catch and translate messages your body is telling you. This practice will ease your mind, taking it from confusion to clarity. You will translate the body's message to the mind in a way it can receive it, an intuitive way versus willing the mind or deceiving it. This practice can benefit you in every area of your life.

In the next chapter, I tell the story of how I discovered, piece by piece, this innate body-based intelligence that changed my life and the lives of thousands of people.

CHAPTER 2

THE MAKING OF WHOLE BODY INTELLIGENCE

You can't connect the dots looking forward; you can only connect them looking backwards. So you have to trust that the dots will somehow connect in your future. You have to trust in something—your gut, destiny, life, karma, whatever. The approach has never let me down, and it has made all the difference in my life.

—STEVE JOBS

COLLEGE PARK, MARYLAND. MAY 5, 1970. The day after the Kent State shootings. Four students dead, nine wounded. We all watched the news footage the night before, over and over. There are more antiwar demonstrations planned in high schools, colleges, and universities around the country. It is quiet at my school this evening.

I have a test in my mass communications class tomorrow, so I make my way from my dorm to the university library, find a quiet cubicle, and pull out my copy of *The Hidden Persuaders* by Vance Packard. His exposé of the subliminal tactics used by supermarket chains and fast-food restaurants is getting me riled up. I am reading about the tricks supermarkets employ to compel us to buy more and how fast-food chains play up-tempo music so we will chew faster and hurry on out. My chest tightens noticeably. I am angry. I feel duped.

All of a sudden, the hush of the library is broken by the sound of chairs squeaking and scraping across the floor. I hear a woman's voice shout, "It's the National Guard. They have tear gas. Let's get out of here!"

All around me students are running, books in hand, throwing their backpacks over their shoulders, rushing toward the front door. I grab my belongings and make my own exodus out the side door onto the quadrangle. A large grassy area where students congregate or just hang out and relax, the quad is in the center of four Southern mansions that accommodate university classrooms. It is a warm spring evening, but there is a ghostly, unnatural feeling in the air.

My thoughts bounce around like a pinball. "Am I going to get teargassed? What about my exam tomorrow? When will they end the war in Vietnam?" The anger I feel suddenly becomes intensely personal. I see a wave of people running toward University Avenue, and I follow. My anger escalates into rage when I hear police sirens and see smoke and fire up ahead. I move in closer to the action, not sure what to do or which way to go. I approach the crowd; a National Guardsman walks straight toward me. Freeze frame. I cannot believe what I'm seeing—I know the guy. His name is John. We sat next to one another in high school science class. We stare each other up and down. He is wearing combat fatigues and a belt of tear gas pellets and has a rifle slung over his shoulder. I stand before him. I am wearing bell-bottom jeans and a flannel shirt and have a backpack full of books slung over my shoulder. Neither of us utters a word.

He turns and runs toward the crowd. I know from his gait that he's been well trained for the job he's about to do.

I drop to the ground, stunned. All of the anger I'd been feeling a few moments before drains out of my body and into the grass.

When I stand up, I'm disoriented, unsure where to go or what to think. I walk toward Harford Hall, my dormitory, but am hesitant about being alone. As I pass the student union, I decide to get a slice of pizza and hope to see someone I know. I walk toward the cafeteria, and a bright yellow poster on the main bulletin board catches my eye. The bold headline reads, "Celebrations of Life." I read down further—the event is hosted by the Reverend David Loomis, a Harvard graduate in human development. The words *human development* pique my interest. The event is being held at the university chapel, and it started 15 minutes ago. It's just what I need—a sanctuary where I can regroup before I go back to my dorm room.

I enter the building. A chill runs up and down my spine when I read the bronze plaque before me on the wall. "Dedicated in 1952 as a living memorial to members of the University community who gave their lives in times of war." The paradox slaps me in the face: Here I am, an antiwar supporter, looking for refuge from a war protest turned riot, and I'm standing in a living memorial to fallen soldiers.

I walk into the chapel and take a seat. The young chaplain

gestures and directs me to join the students sitting on the floor near the altar. I wonder, "What kind of service has people sitting on the floor?"

I sit down cross-legged like everyone else. They all have their eyes closed, and they are making a sound I've never heard before. Rev. Loomis explains, "What you're hearing is *Om*, the primordial sound of the universe. Chanting Om invokes peace."

I'm thinking, "Have I just walked into an episode of *The Twilight Zone*? Is this really happening? A war, shootings, and riots . . . and now you're telling me the way to peace is by making this odd sound?"

Rev. Loomis directs us to concentrate on our breath: "Breathe in slow and deep, in through the nose, out through the mouth, making the sound of om as you exhale." I feel self-conscious and awkward, but within a few moments I notice that my body really likes this. Another 3 or 4 minutes pass. The reverberation of the om has allowed my mind to slow down—way down. I feel more relaxed than I've ever felt before. My lungs and chest feel expansive. I am no longer afraid or confused. My body is humming with new energy.

An hour later I leave the chapel in what Rev. Loomis termed an "altered state," thinking, "I was looking for refuge and peace, but had no idea that I would find what I was seeking inside of me."

CONNECTING THE DOTS . . .

That eventful afternoon and evening changed the direction of my life. The combination of a real threat to my physical well-being, an encounter with a high school classmate turned National Guardsman, and stumbling into a state of deep peace brought about by concentrating on my breathing and making a mystical sound was an initiation. I didn't know it at the time, and wouldn't connect the dots until many years later, but I had stepped onto a new path and entered a new relationship with myself. A seed was planted that would continue to grow and lead me all the way to creating the Whole Body Intelligence program and this book.

Josephine Hart, in her 1991 novel turned film, *Damage*, said, "There is an internal landscape, a geography of the soul; we search for its outlines all our lives." I can fully relate to what Hart was saying. After my Celebrations of Life experience, I maintained an active academic and social life, but I was now running on an important parallel track, my inner inquiry, at the same time.

Within a matter of months, I'd submerged myself in the study of the mind, the body, and this unusual state of inner stillness Rev. Loomis had termed an altered state. This state seemed to me far more stable and real—as a state of being— than the mind could obtain when left to its own devices. Once I'd embarked on this inner adventure and glimpsed the vast territory contained there, I was in. I had to explore and traverse every corner of the landscape.

. . . LED TO YES!

When I got back to my dorm after the Celebrations of Life at the chapel, I learned that the university president had canceled classes for the next 4 days. I took advantage of this unexpected break (and postponement of the test) to make the first leg of what would turn out to be a lifelong journey.

The following morning I got in my gold Ford Mustang and headed south. I'd heard about a metaphysical bookstore in Washington, DC, and hoped to find some books that would inform my new interest.

I walked through the door of the bookstore and was met by the sweet, pungent fragrances of incense and aromatherapy oils. Ambient music played softly in the background. I looked around at the colorful displays: tarot cards, crystals, pendulums, and sage wands. I'd never seen anything like it. I walked over to the bookshelves; the categories—metaphysics, inspirational, spiritual, Taoism, self-help—were unfamiliar and yet intriguing.

I was drawn to a book with a bright orange cover and a photo of a long-haired Indian man, Paramahansa Yogananda's *Autobiography of a Yogi*. Yogananda's life story is full of miraculous stories that chronicle his encounters with the sages, gurus, and sadhus of India. The book is a primer on Kriya Yoga—a meditation practice that leads to states of tranquillity and profound self-awareness. I read the book twice and knew I had to learn yoga and meditation.

Three months later, after a summer trip to Europe and the Middle East with a friend, I was back on campus. On the first day of classes, I ran into an old friend, Mike, whom I hadn't seen in a while. He seemed different; his eyes were unusually clear and, I kid you not, the glow around him was palpable. He told me he'd just returned from a trip to Colorado, where he'd met a young Indian teacher who taught him a meditation practice that he called *knowledge.* He went on to share that he felt much happier and calmer now that he was sitting to meditate two or three times a day.

The next night Mike invited me to hear more about his experience. We went to a beautiful Victorian private home on Dupont Circle in Washington, DC. The hosts, like Mike, were new students of Prem Pal Singh Rawat, a 14-year-old boy known to his students as Guru Maharaj Ji. One at a time they shared how their lives had changed since receiving knowledge. I was keen to note how authentic they seemed, and it wasn't just their words; it was what they communicated through their bodies as well. I saw in them a kind of ease and congruence that I wanted. A few weeks later, I attended a larger event with Maharaj Ji and his mahatmas, or teachers. I was impressed that these teachers were not selling meditation; the teachings were offered at no cost to those who aspired to develop a meditation practice that would bring happiness.

In the weeks and months that followed, I meditated for many hours. The meditation technique proved quite valuable; I had a practice I could turn to that allowed me to listen to what was going on inside of me. The benefits were immediately noticeable; I was less stressed and had a new ability to monitor and control the reactive patterns in my mind.

Game on. Just as the British invasion had brought the Beatles and dozens of other mop-haired pop bands across the Atlantic the decade before, the Indian teachers were marching right into the hearts and minds of Americans with inner music. The Yes! Bookshop hosted these teachers, one after another, every week.

One evening I met a teacher who wore all orange—his shirt, his pants—even his bright knit hat. I was told that he was a swami; one who serves others without expecting any reward. They wear orange to symbolize the sun—the Self—shining selflessly onto the world. Another person told me that the saffron orange clothes are a reminder that we each possess the fire that can burn away any hardship.

Our speaker for the night was introduced as Swami Muktananda, whose name means "the Bliss of Freedom." He talked about Siddha Yoga, a spiritual path that holds that what we truly are—beyond the mind, body, and ego—is divinity. He gave us *shaktipat,* an energy transmission that awakens the kundalini—the divine power and potential that lies sleeping in the human organism. Siddha Yoga teaches that when this energy gets awakened, it sets us on the path of spiritual awareness and unlimited possibilities. Kundalini is often represented as a snake that is coiled up at the base of the spine. Teachers like Muktananda, or "Baba," as his students called him, teach how to unwind that coiled-up energy so that it moves freely.

When it was my turn to receive *shaktipat,* Baba gazed in my eyes and pressed on my forehead. I saw a burst of light appear between my eyes; for the next 30 minutes, I felt energy moving up and down my spine. I was intrigued and wanted to learn more about how to take charge of my own "blocked" energy and release my potential.

By this time I was in graduate school studying communications at American University in Washington, DC. Meeting various teachers became a regular, weekly activity—I was a full-time student. I attended American University to earn a master's degree and went to locations like Yes! Bookshop to learn how to master my "inner" abilities.

I studied teachers like Sri Swami Satchidananda, the founder of Integral Yoga. He blended the physical discipline of yoga, the spiritual philosophy of India, and an innovative interfaith approach that promoted harmony within. By making yoga accessible to millions, he helped launch and shape the modern yoga movement that has since become a global phenomenon. His essential teaching is captured on the wall at Yogaville, his center in Buckingham County, Virginia. It reads:

> This goal [reaching harmony and peace within] is achieved by maintaining our natural condition of a body of optimum health and strength, senses under total control, a mind well-disciplined, clear and calm, an intellect as sharp as a razor, a will as strong and pliable as steel, a heart full of unconditional love and compassion, an ego as pure as a crystal, and a life filled with Supreme Peace and Joy.

I also attended trainings with Pir Vilayat Inayat Khan, who was head of the Sufi Order in the West. Khan taught me a meditation practice wherein I focused on seven energy centers, or chakras, that sat along the central axis of the body near the spine.

By now my life and understanding of myself was taking a big U-turn. To borrow the words of physicist Fred Alan Wolf, PhD ("Dr. Quantum" in the 2004 film *What the #$*! Do We [K]now!?*): "What I thought was unreal . . . now for me seems in some ways to be more real . . . than what I think to be real . . . which seems now, more to be unreal."

Every experience showed me something new about myself. Although I didn't know it at the time, I was gathering a valuable collection of techniques and insights that I would apply to my life and work one day.

I dove into the study of body language, psychology, spirituality, and just about anything that related to human well-being, happiness, and success. I studied and practiced various spiritual teachings and methods, both ancient and modern.

As my own self-awareness increased, many things began falling into place. I became clearer about my own gifts and my calling in life.

BE HERE NOW

On one of my many treks to the Yes! Bookshop, I came upon an unusual-looking book called *Be Here Now* written by Richard Alpert, PhD, a Harvard psychiatrist who went to India seeking deeper meaning for his life. The book is an account of Dr. Alpert's metamorphosis into Baba Ram Dass.

I had never seen a book like this before. Instead of the usual white paper and standard book size, this book was square, printed on brown paper, and full of rich artwork, roughly drawn cartoons, and short statements—profound truths about what it means to "be here now." When I saw that Ram Dass was coming to town, I bought a ticket.

He began his talk saying that Ram stood for "rent a mouth," since he loved to meet and share his findings with others. I loved his humorous approach to self-awareness and felt especially inspired when he read this from his book: "One can share a message through telling our story as I have just done, or through the teaching methods of Yoga, or singing, or making love. Each of us finds his unique vehicle for sharing with others his bit of wisdom. For me this story is but a vehicle for sharing with you the true message . . . the living faith in what is possible."

I was about to graduate from American University; it was the perfect time for me to hear his message. Ram Dass spoke of *right livelihood,* which inspired to me to incorporate my internal and external skills in my professional life. I decided to open an advertising firm to serve clients and organizations I believed in. I wanted to work with people who had a valuable message, to help them communicate that message to others.

My business grew quickly. I started with clients I already knew: the owner of a restaurant I frequented, and friends who owned a clothing boutique. I worked out of a small, one-room office with one very talented graphic artist named Leo. Within 12 months, the Procom Group had grown to a nine-person staff in a suite of offices in the prestigious Chevy Chase Building on Wisconsin Avenue in Chevy Chase, Maryland. It was a perfect location for acquiring clients in Maryland, the District of Columbia, and Virginia. I was on purpose.

I met with clients, radio and TV salespeople, and commercial producers throughout the day. In the evening I meditated and did yoga. By now I was starting to get very comfortable with the myriad practices I learned and was achieving very relaxed and elevated states. After my "time inside," I would create and script campaigns for my clients. I wrote radio and TV commercials, music jingles, and even speeches for political candidates. Achieving success, building client and staff relationships, and expressing my creativity to get results for others felt great. I decided, no matter what, that whatever I was destined to do in the years to come, I would express my gifts and help others. I am pleased to share that is exactly what I do in my work today.

WHAT'S YOUR BODY TELLING YOU?

After several years of success, I started to yearn for more. I began to get restless while at the office. Acquiring new clients and creating ads wasn't doing it for me anymore.

One day in a TV production studio, I was watching a client deliver words I'd written for him a few nights earlier. I recall the vision I had of him in a meditation. He stood tall and seemed genuinely relaxed and confident as he looked into the camera. He believed in his audio store and the products and services he offered, and that certainty came right through his eyes to the viewer. Between what I knew about his dedication to customers and my clever words, I recognized a grand-slam home run for this ad campaign. However, when the lights came up and the cameras began to roll, I saw a man who was perspiring heavily and crunching his body forward. He was anything but relaxed and confident. I knew the problem wasn't the words I'd written for him, it was how he was saying those words. His mouth and his body were speaking entirely different languages.

I called time-out and privately asked my client to listen to what his body was telling him as he practiced reciting the script. Each time he read it, I asked, "What's your body telling you?" After several run-throughs, he started noticing his posture and breathing as he delivered his message. This added awareness on his part helped him get over the jitters and relax his body. As we filmed the next take, I noticed how authentic he looked when he spoke. I believed him this time! In the end the campaign was a big success.

After seeing how my client transformed right in front of my eyes, I was hooked. I continued to run the agency, but my passion became coaching clients on their delivery. I felt more like a movie director than a script writer for TV commercials. Every time I got a client to "feel" the words in their body rather than just say the words, their delivery became spot-on. They were able to communicate their message in a powerful and authentic way, and viewers responded. I would often tell them, "Your body is your billboard. Stay aware of what message it is broadcasting to your marketplace."

This was the launchpad for what I am doing today: helping clients and organizations discover their blind spots and correct them for better results. I am always amazed that life knows where it is taking us even when we don't.

What I did know was that the ad game had grown stale. Recently married, my wife and I were tired of East Coast winters and wanted to grow organic food year-round, so I sold my agency and we moved south and landed just outside Tampa, Florida.

The next 4 years were a gestation period. I immersed myself further into explorations of the body through gardening, yoga, and swimming in the warm, spring-fed lake behind our home.

I went on 7- and 10-day juice fasts and raw food diets. My body felt relaxed and energized at the same. We taught beginners' yoga at several recreation centers and planted and farmed a huge organic garden. Teaching yoga and gardening every day kept me in touch with my body. My days of sitting behind a desk were over.

I opened an organic juice bar next to the University of Tampa campus and, from that customer base, built a large sales network for our Shaklee vitamins and biodegradable products business. I developed valuable sales, presentation, and people skills both in the juice bar and while leading Shaklee sales meetings. I also spent even more time on self-exploration and introspection. The combination made me much happier with myself and, in turn, brought success. My wife and I were among the top 20 sales producers and were asked to speak at a Shaklee convention in New Orleans.

Once again I was sensing that the success I was having was directly related to the amount of time and attention I put on learning to understand and manage me, from the inside out.

MY NEXT TEACHER ARRIVES

*Just as there is no warning for childbirth, there
is no preparation for the sight of a first child.
But perhaps there is none because there are no words
strong enough to name the moment.*

—ANITA DIAMANT, *THE RED TENT*

When my wife got pregnant, we decided we wanted to have a natural childbirth. We'd heard about a French obstetrician,

Dr. Fernand Lamaze, who popularized a method where couples trained together for the birth. During our first Lamaze class, I was excited when the teacher informed us we would be using a combination of breathing, movement, and massage during labor. Then we read Frédérick Leboyer, MD's book *Birth without Violence*. We knew immediately that we wanted this type of birth: a dimly lit room, an easy transition from the womb, and immediate bonding like putting our newborn on his mother's stomach rather than handing him off to a nurse to be weighed and measured.

In 1971 Ina May Gaskin, along with her late husband, Stephen, had founded the Farm, the longest running American commune that still operates to this day. Located near the town of Summertown, Tennessee, Ina May and her team of midwives restored the birth process to its rightful place in the hands and arms of women. We found a copy of one of the Farm's first publications and read the section on natural childbirth over and over. The whole idea of trusting in the ancient wisdom of the body reinforced what I had been discovering for myself over the years.

When Jesse arrived he weighed 7 pounds, 8 ounces and had the biggest, brightest blue eyes I had ever seen. He was also very alert—no need to spank this little guy to wake him up. His mom held him close to her heart, and he began to breast-feed right away. The peace on his face, the miracle I had just witnessed, these are forever etched in my heart.

It didn't take long to realize that he was my next teacher. For hours I would sit and watch the effortless movement of his diaphragm—rhythmic and consistent. His engine hummed. I compared this to the way most adults breathe and wondered how something so basic as the constant rhythms of breath got so tweaked. I set out to learn everything I could about this basic function that sustains us and, when freed from conditioned restrictions, feeds our mental, physical, and emotional well-being. I'm still on that journey and always will be.

GO WEST, YOUNG MAN

Jesse was 3 years old when three men stopped by our lakeside home unannounced and knocked on the door. They handed me a petition with some 30 to 40 signatures that asked us to move out of "their neighborhood." We didn't know if they were opposed to our religion or lifestyle or both. The men let me know that they'd be back if we didn't move in the next few months.

That visit from the unwelcome wagon was just the nudge we needed. I'd visited San Francisco several times on business and felt certain it was a place I could flourish. It was the nexus of the budding consciousness movement—a place where art, music, and multicultural lifestyles were embraced and celebrated.

Two months later I left the Florida countryside and flew out to San Francisco ahead of my family, intent on finding a job. On day 1 I rented us a home in Marin County, just north of the Golden Gate Bridge. On day 2 I took possession of the house and bought a couple of beds for the family and a new suit and tie for me. On day 3 I cut my hair and scanned the classified ads in the *San Francisco Chronicle*. By midafternoon, I had made a decision: to find a lucrative sales job. I needed to be in charge of my own schedule to make time for family and other interests.

On day 4, while walking around the Financial District in downtown San Francisco wearing my new duds and killing time before an interview, my mind made a full frontal assault: "You never should have left Florida. The gall of those people calling it 'their neighborhood'! Did I act too impulsively? What if I can't find a job?" After about 30 minutes of spinning around in my head, I sat down on a bench in a grassy area, closed my eyes, and took a number of slow, deep breaths. A warm, calm feeling washed over me. My whole body relaxed. Underneath the turbulence of my mind was a calm knowing; I was sitting in the perfect place to build a future for my family. I'd been in Northern California for less than a week. Everywhere I went, the scenery, the people, the open-hearted welcome—it all felt so right. Sitting in that park in the midst of a cluster of high-rise office buildings, I knew the move to SF had a deeper purpose; this was a fertile place to raise my son, apply my people skills, delve deeper into consciousness studies, and grow in new directions.

That afternoon I was hired as a sales representative for a leading business equipment corporation. I woke up the next day feeling energized—my sense of purpose was palpable. Driving over the Golden Gate Bridge, I was enveloped in the fluffy fog of the San Francisco Bay. It was a spiritual experience. I felt I had found my home.

Every day on my commute across the Golden Gate Bridge, I did breathing exercises and sang. By the time I walked in the office, I was fired up to connect with people. Right away I saw how my years of "inner training" gave me a leg up—I was able to connect with customers on an authentic level. One thing became apparent on sales calls: The connection I could make with people from a grounded place inside myself was more important than the company and products I represented. I thought about my advertising days, how clients communicated micromessages through their body and the effect that had on sales. I observed my body language in every appointment. I learned that when I leaned forward, my customer would back up. When I would take a deep, quiet breath and relax my shoulders, my customers would follow suit. My sales strategy became clear. Before I walked into an appointment, I took a few minutes to relax and scan my body for any tension. In the actual appointment, I stayed aware of my body language and remained attentive to my customer's body while presenting my product line.

Buyers often complimented me on my confidence in my product and myself. Unlike other sales reps, I watched who talked nervously and didn't really listen, and I was able to stay engaged. My body matched my words. What they experienced was congruency, which fed and enhanced my confidence. This became a winning combination for me. Within a month I was the number two sales producer in the western region. Shortly thereafter I was ranked at the top of a national sales force of 500, and I remained in that spot for several years. To this day, when I address sales organizations, I show them my secret to success: Increase self-awareness and improve listening skills.

In the fourth year of working for my company, I received a promotion to national accounts manager. Along with servicing my accounts, I was asked to train sales personnel as well. To me this meant I could create a program based on the best techniques and practices I'd learned over the years and watch what results it got for others. The results were impressive. One hundred percent of the salespeople who followed the program reported increased productivity, a clearer focus, and higher sales.

The higher-ups at the home office asked me to move to Hartford, Connecticut, to be the director of training. They assured me this would be a direct route to the VP of sales position in the future. I did the math—some of the megasize accounts I'd developed were buying up to 3,000 machines a year. The director of sales position might be more prestigious, but I didn't want to take the pay cut, didn't want to leave San Francisco, and felt perfectly happy where I was.

A stone-faced head honcho from the corporate office came to SF with a different take. He implied that as a company man I should be thrilled to rise up the organization's ladder. He wondered it if was time for me to move on. I sensed, underneath everything he said, that it was not an option for me to continue earning more out in the field than some of the executives at the home office pulled in.

Again I saw this as a sign to move forward. It was time for me to teach my as-yet-unnamed peak performance program on my own.

I spent the next 30 days turning my accounts over to other reps, saying my good-byes, and clearing out my desk. I decided to take some time off before I made my next move. My wife and I had grown apart and divorced. It was time to regroup.

MY COMING-OUT PARTY

I went to Glen Ivy, aka "Club Mud"—a hot springs spa near Corona, California. Glen Ivy is known for its red clay mud; the spa's specialty is a combination of red clay and geothermic mineral water that draws away toxins and dead skin cells and revitalizes the body. I was ready to shed my old skin and spent a week applying mud and soaking while looking at what my life might look like in the days ahead. Sitting in 104°F pools beneath the Santa Ana Mountains, looking out at the majestic views of the Temescal Valley, was one the best things I ever did for myself. I was starting to feel my body clear the stress of leaving my job and ending a marriage.

On my fifth day at Club Mud, I asked myself a question: What is missing in Marin County that I could provide? I went through a menu of items and one popped up the loudest— networking. There were no regular networking events in the county. The lightbulb flashed brightly and my energy rose, just like it had when I landed my corporate sales job. That familiar sense of purpose and a "yes!" in my gut confirmed that I was going to create the largest and coolest networking event Marin County had ever seen. I thought, "I've spent the past 6 years working in San Francisco. Now I can meet businesspeople in my backyard and they'll come to me instead of me constantly prospecting and following up on leads." Once again energy ran up and down my spine, and I felt as though I'd received *shaktipat*. I couldn't wait to get home and execute the idea.

When I came home, I went to Sarkey's, a popular restaurant in Sausalito. It was the perfect location, close to San Francisco, to bring people from the city and Marin together. I told Mr. Sarkey about my idea and guaranteed to bring in a crowd to fill his bar and upstairs disco on the slowest night of the week. He gave me a couple Mondays; it was up to me to fill the room. There was no Internet, no e-mail, no Instagram, no Facebook or Twitter, and no Craigslist, so my social media campaign consisted of a flyer and whomever I gave it to. I walked into offices and chambers of commerce throughout the county, inviting people to come network and dance. Two hundred and forty people attended the first Marin Business Exchange. I greeted each person at the front door, saying, "Welcome. I'm Steve Sisgold; here's my card. Call me if you want to know how to realize your dreams." I set nine appointments that night. When I got home and reflected on what had just happened, I had two thoughts: "I did it. I launched my practice," and "What am I going to do when they come in for a session?"

WATCHING THE POWER OF WBI UNFOLD

I began the first session by asking my client what he desired in his personal and business life. As he shared what his dream job and relationship would look like, and told me his immediate goal was meeting his sales quota for the year, I noticed that his voice rose an octave and his body started shaking. I asked him to say his desire aloud again several times and let his body do whatever it wanted to do. I remember saying, "Let your body move, talk, and make sounds. It seems to have something to tell you." He looked at me a bit strangely and said, "I thought I was coming for advice on how to meet my quota this year." I assured him that was exactly what we were going to do, that I was just the facilitator, and that his body had the information he needed.

Fifteen minutes of breathing and bringing awareness into his body, and he started shaking. Tears came up. He said, "I had no idea that telling you what I want would bring up such a strong reaction in my body." He'd accessed past memories and fears that he felt could be stopping his success. Bingo. I knew exactly what my private practice would focus on after that session.

I continued to ask people what they desired and gave them feedback on what I noticed. I also taught them breathing exercises and encouraged them to let their body talk until an insight came forward. I offered encouragement to express and move the energy that felt stuck in their body in order to free themselves from whatever was holding them back, not just mentally but physically.

I knew I was on to something, although I didn't know exactly how or why it worked.

I helped an award-winning songwriter uncover and change a limiting belief that caused writer's block. When he discovered this limiting belief buried deep in his body memory, he began to change it and, in short order, started writing again.

A bestselling author wanted to get on *Oprah* and other big TV shows. In our sessions he released a hand-me-down family belief that he carried in his body. After clearing this belief and embodying a more positive one in its place, he approached the same TV producers and got a very different result—he was booked on national TV.

A CEO was having debilitating anxiety. He could not relax when he wasn't at the office. Within weeks he was managing his stress and enjoying his home life with his family.

A physician referred a patient suffering from stomach pain for many months. She discovered she was squeezing in deep-seated anger about how she was being treated at work. When she let her belly relax and expressed her anger, her pain went away.

I was a teacher and a student, learning more about what I was doing in each session. I was astounded by the body's intelligence and what it revealed when it was listened to.

I wanted to know more and was drawn to others doing similar mind-body integration work in what was emerging as the new field of somatics, a term coined by Thomas Hanna, PhD. Derived from the Greek word *somatikos* (*soma*: living, aware, bodily person), somatics means "pertaining to the body, experienced and regulated from within." Dr. Hanna defined somatics as the study of self from the perspective of one's lived experience, encompassing the dimensions of body, psyche, and spirit. Dr. Hanna's work addressed what he called sensory motor amnesia—in everyday terms, the muscles have forgotten how to move without the restriction. His somatics addresses this by retraining the body to move freely and naturally through neuromuscular (mind-body) movement education.

While Dr. Hanna was chairman of philosophy at the University of Florida, he discovered the work of Moshe Feldenkrais, an Israeli man who'd received his doctor of science degree from the Sorbonne. Dr. Feldenkrais had also studied jujitsu for a number of years and was told by Jigoro Kano, the founder of judo, that he would be an important doorway for the East to meet the West. While Dr. Feldenkrais was serving in the war, he aggravated an old soccer injury but refused to have the recommended knee surgery. He chose instead to self-rehabilitate by observing his movement very carefully, which led him to develop the Feldenkrais Method. When Dr. Hanna met Dr. Feldenkrais, he was impressed by the work, as it was in tune with his philosophy. By then Dr. Hanna had become the director of the Humanistic Psychology Institute (now the Saybrook Institute). In 1975 Dr. Hanna hosted the first Feldenkrais training in the United States.

What I learned about these two pioneers inspired me to refine my own method. I began to offer a two-part session. Half of the hour would be a somatics inquiry to learn what memories lived on in the body and held people back. The next half hour involved helping clients become congruent to communicate their message authentically from head to toe, just as I'd done when training salespeople. I created a niche that appealed to people who were looking for both.

About that time, Gay Hendricks, PhD, and Kathlyn Hendricks, PhD, bestselling self-help authors, came for a weekend intensive. They were two of the most vibrant and brilliant people I'd ever met. They were pioneering new paths in body-centered therapy, couples communication, and what they called Radiance Breathwork. They wanted to grow their institute and were unclear how to do that. When they saw that my approach began in the body, they were confident they'd come to the right place. They got great results from our sessions, and we decided to work together. I was invited to teach my manifestation work in their trainings. I watched and experienced firsthand how the breath work and movement protocols they had developed accelerated breakthroughs for people. Together we made a great team helping people who were blocked by self-imposed limitations and subconscious or unconscious patterns identify and release them.

These were important formative years for both my personal development and the formation of WBI. The Drs. Hendricks and I held several joint events in the Bay Area, and Gay and I created and facilitated the (W)inner Circle, a 2-year program designed to support participants to manifest their dreams. We worked with 27 hand-picked folks and met quarterly in San Francisco, Chicago, and Santa Barbara. It was the ultimate laboratory for me to test WBI practices. Working with the same people over a 24-month period allowed me to track their progress and see what worked and what didn't. The results for every one of us were outstanding, and for me quite transformational.

In one session I revealed that even though I appeared to be a mellow guy, I'd been struggling inwardly for decades. I could not release the trauma of learning about the Holocaust as a young, impressionable kid. Whenever I saw a movie or writings about the Holocaust, I would feel intense rage coupled with an urge to strike back. I was able to control myself, but I knew I was pushing down feelings that had to be expressed. I'd never revealed this to any but a few very close friends, much less before a group of people. It felt scary, but I told the (W)inner Circle about my issue and my plan to change it . . . and about the day my childhood innocence got taken away.

I'd been sent to the store on a bread-and-pickle run. I grabbed a loaf of still-warm bread and dashed toward the deli counter to get the pickles when I saw a lady from our neighborhood. I'd seen her before and had been puzzled why everyone called her a "refugee." I didn't know what *refugee* meant, but I knew she was different from the rest of the people I knew. She spoke a language I did not understand and always seemed sad.

Normally this woman was all covered up, from top to bottom, but it was a typical Baltimore hot and humid day, so her sleeves were rolled up. I saw bluish green numbers branded on her lower arm. My breath caught in my throat. I froze for a minute, then ran as hard as I could to get out of there. I made record time on my run home and asked my mother what the numbers meant. The uncomfortable look on her face was familiar—I'd seen it before—but that day my discomfort was stronger than hers and I would not relent until she explained. That was the day the words *Nazi* and *Holocaust* became part of my vocabulary. I was told by my mom to never think or talk about it again.

When I shared this story with the (W)inner Circle, I also shared my decision to travel to Germany and Poland to trace my roots and heal the hurt and rage in my body. The circle members responded by offering a tremendous amount of empathy and encouragement.

On the last day of our week together, Gay asked if he could join me on my trip, then several members of our circle offered us the funds to document our journey on film so we could share our experience with others. I named the film *Loosening the Grip* to emphasize one of the main themes: the importance of feeling the grip of unresolved emotional reactions as they manifest in the body and expressing those feelings with the conscious intention to heal.

Auschwitz, Poland

When we walked into the barracks in the Birkenau concentration camp, minutes from the Auschwitz camp, my eyes went directly to a bank of wooden planks fastened to the wall. We were told this is where the savage medical experiments took place. Four or five people had been required to lie on each plank, awaiting their death. I was stunned. I lay down on one of the bunks and fell silent. My mind couldn't begin to comprehend what had occurred there. I kept repeating "How could this happen?" over and over until I finally managed to get up and walk out of the barracks.

I looked across the yard and felt the urge to run. My body was flooded with adrenaline as I bolted across the muddy field toward the prison watchtower. A fierce, animal instinct took over and I leapt into the air. Forty years of held-down ferocity slammed into the watchtower. One of the wood pilings cracked.

I stepped back and began to scream and rage and yell and cry and scream and yell and rage and cry. All the fear and confusion, the bitterness and mistrust that had kept me from feeling my rage began to surface. I didn't hold anything back. When it was over, a feeling of peace settled into my body. I returned to the States determined to help others embrace their hurts and clear distressing memories that lived on in their bodies; to help them express, transform, and release the vital energy that was blocked by events in the past, like I did.

My son was off to college in San Diego, so I went to Maui, my favorite Hawaiian island. It was time to reboot. I'd planned to hunker down, to write the script and edit the hundreds of hours shot in Berlin and Auschwitz. After that I would write a book. I thought I'd stay on Maui a year, but it turned out to be 5. Between writing the script and watching dozens of hours of footage over and over, the healing continued. The more I expressed my feelings, the more the hold the Holocaust had on me loosened. I felt lighter and freer. I will always honor the people who suffered and died there and feel my grief about that, but facing my anger and making the film relieved me of the intense rage I carried. I also learned an important lesson: Immersing oneself in a creative project that focuses on lingering past hurts is a powerful way to heal.

THE MARRIAGE OF
HEALING AND CREATIVITY CONTINUES

Next I wanted to write a book. I was sitting on the beach thinking about how to begin it. Nothing came for hours, so I decided to put on fins and a snorkel and go for a swim. Between breathing deeply and listening to the sound of my breath under water, I dropped into a trance. I closed my eyes and knew how to open the book.

I saw the opening scene vividly: I was 11 years old. I had a crew cut, but the front of my hair was longer and stood straight up from "butch wax." ("Wow" is all I can say about that.)

We'd just sat down for family dinner when my father announced, "Midget Grocery downtown is up for sale. I want to buy it." He might as well have told us that we were going to pack up the house and move to Iceland. I looked across the table at my mother; her face went through at least six different emotions in rapid succession before she regained control of her vocal cords: "What? You can't quit your job! Don't be ridiculous, Morris. That is the craziest thing I've ever heard."

My father had always been a good provider. He held a management position at an established grocery chain and brought home a dependable salary. Security was a high value in our house, and my mother argued convincingly against my father's outlandish idea. The risks definitely outweighed the benefits: end of story.

I looked back and forth across the table, watching carefully to see what came next. My heart was singing in response to the excitement I'd heard in my father's announcement. More than once he'd talked about running his own business. This was his dream. How could my mom not see that?

My thoughts ran wild: "Don't interrupt, or you'll be in trouble. Keep quiet; it's none of my business; I'm just a kid; what do I know? They won't listen to me anyway." But my heart felt like it was about to jump right out of my chest. The censor in my mind didn't have a chance.

A feeling of certainty moved through me, but my mouth had already started to speak: "Dad! Get the store! You can do it, I know you can!"

The following day my dad took my mother to see Midget Grocery. She walked into the place and within 5 minutes changed her mind; she wanted my dad to buy the store.

It wasn't long before my dad became the proud owner of Super Discount Grocery Store and hosted a grand opening celebration. Within a matter of weeks, the local supermarkets closed due to a statewide strike. Overnight, Super Discount became the go-to place for a hungry neighborhood. For weeks people lined up around the block to buy groceries. Many of them became regulars at the store.

For me it was a marker moment. I'd broken the rules. I'd acted on the feeling of conviction—the impassioned certainty— that flashed through my body at that dinner table. I couldn't possibly have put into words what happened that day. Only decades later when I looked back did the pivotal nature of that experience become clear. It was the first time in conscious memory that Whole Body Intelligence asserted authority in my life. I wasn't aware of it at the time, but that event, and the boon it became for my family right away, fundamentally changed me. I was a different person than I'd been before. A kind of knowledge beyond the jurisdiction of reason had been revealed to me. Revisiting that time and other past events through the writing of my book connected even more dots for me toward my personal healing and the importance of sharing my work.

Within a short time I was selling my book, *What's Your*

Body Telling You?, which introduced some of my concepts to the world.

In the years since, I have brought my body-first approach to entrepreneurs, top executives, and high-performance teams. I've trained physicians, health practitioners, coaches, and therapists in the WBI method. Each client, each training, and each situation has helped me hone and refine what is now the WBI program, which consists of core insights and practices to destress on demand, transform limiting beliefs, and create lasting change.

The thread that weaves through my story and ties everything together is a willingness and natural ability to listen to my body and follow its guidance. I resisted at times, of course. Like so many young boys, I'd been conditioned to ignore feelings and my body. Nonetheless, whenever I did listen, when I took that leap and followed the whispers, I found myself on solid ground. My body took me where I was supposed to go.

Follow your body where it takes you, and connect the dots of your own life story, as together we enter the next stage of our journey: movement awareness.

CHAPTER 3

HOW DO YOU MOVE THROUGH LIFE?

A living body is not a fixed thing but a flowing event,
like a flame or a whirlpool.

—ALAN WATTS

RIGHT NOW, WHETHER YOU are aware of it or not, your body is adjusting to meet the demands of the moment. That might mean shifting positions in your seat to get more comfortable, turning the page of this book when you are ready, or reaching for your water bottle because you are thirsty. Your body is intelligent enough to react and adjust, refine and habituate, and find some semblance of balance in any scenario. Your body is always doing its thing, whether you choose to listen to it or not.

What's miraculous about us as human beings is that we have the ability to make a choice in every moment, to adapt and move with our body or to ignore, resist, or even move against it.

In the previous chapters, you discovered and experienced the body-first approach: choosing to listen to your body, before your mind, for immediate feedback on your experience. You gained some understanding of the value of this approach and the benefits it offers. You are now far more likely to notice when your breathing becomes shallow or your jaw is clamped tight before a business meeting or other life event. Moreover, you know to listen to the tight feeling in your stomach before you reply yes or no to an invitation. You also learned that your body has a built-in alert system that warns you when you're about to make an unhealthy decision.

In this chapter you will explore another dimension of body intelligence: movement awareness. You'll discover the link between your body movements and unconscious patterns. You will learn how to catch habitual movements and gestures and make a conscious choice about your next move; default patterns will no longer determine your actions and negatively impact your communication with others. You will uncover movement signatures that may affect how you are perceived and discover what messages you are sending through your body language. And you will learn that movement awareness can actually make you smarter.

CHANGE YOUR MOVEMENT, CHANGE YOUR BRAIN

Being aware of how you move your body can help you think more clearly and turn up the dial on your brainpower. Research shows that the brain can take cues from body movements to understand and solve complex problems.

In 2009 University of Illinois psychology professor Alejandro Lleras, PhD, along with Laura Thomas, PhD, of Vanderbilt

University, conducted a study on problem solving and body movement. They set out to test if a person's ability to solve a complex problem could be influenced by how he or she moves. They tested 52 University of Illinois students. The results showed that body motion affects higher-order thought and complex problem solving.

"People tend to think that their mind lives in their brain, dealing in conceptual abstractions, very much disconnected from the body," Drs. Lleras and Thomas reported. "This emerging research is fascinating because it is demonstrating how your body is a part of your mind in a powerful way. The way you think is affected by your body and, in fact, we can use our bodies to help us think."

This study confirms what I often see in Whole Body Intelligence sessions. Clients will be stuck in some unproductive thought loop or knee-jerk reaction. They become fuzzy and confused as to what is actually occurring right in front of them. I redirect their attention to their body to check if any movements or sensations are happening that they are unaware of. Whether their body is sending a subtle signal or shaking wildly, when they tune in, that attentiveness consistently opens a window to solutions that they didn't get from their mind alone. Clients find that this type of attention shift consistently generates new insight and enhances creative thinking and resiliency. They just seem smarter once they are conscious of how their body moves. Here's why.

Anat Baniel, in her book *Move into Life*, says, "The moment we bring attention to our movements, to any movement, the brain grows a new connection and creates a new neural pathway. Conversely, movement without awareness reinforces the way our neurology is accustomed to doing things—bad patterns and all."

Canadian psychologist Donald Olding Hebb, PhD, is considered the father of neuropsychology. In his classic work of 1949, *The Organization of Behavior*, he writes, "It's important to recognize the inherent power of our neural networks to direct our behavior and our thinking." He goes on to explain, "When an axon of cell A is near enough to excite cell B and repeatedly or persistently takes part in firing it, some growth process or metabolic change takes place in one or both cells such that A's efficiency, as one of the cells firing B, is increased." In plain English, nerve cells that fire together wire together.

In the movie *What the #$*! Do We (K)now!?*, Joe Dispenza, DC, explains this phenomenon this way: "We know physiologically that if you practice something over and over, those nerve cells have a long-term relationship. If you *move* the same way on a daily basis, you're embedding that neural net. And that neural net now has a long-term relationship with all those other nerve cells called an 'identity.' We also know that nerve cells that don't fire together no longer wire together. They lose their long-term relationship because every time we interrupt the thought process that produces a chemical response in the body, those nerve cells that are connected to each other start breaking the long-term relationship."

We are hardwired to use movement awareness to discover and break the neural nets that work against us. Psychiatrist Jeffrey Schwartz, MD, a researcher in the field of neuroplasticity, agrees. In his book *The Mind and the Brain*, he says,

"Humans are *neural electricians*. We can take charge of our brain function. We are not restricted to working with existing wiring. We can run whole new cables through our brain."

DON'T WORRY, BE HAPPY

Along with being smarter, we can create more happiness and less stress through awareness of our body movements, explains social psychologist and Harvard assistant professor Amy Cuddy, PhD. In Dr. Cuddy's TED talk, "Your Body Language Shapes Who You Are," she claims, "Our body language reveals that we can change our own body chemistry—simply by changing body positions." Along with Dana Carney, PhD, associate professor at the University of California, Berkeley, Dr. Cuddy conducted a study called Physical Motion and Performance. They worked with 66 Columbia University students and found that expansive, open movements affect hormone levels. She noted, *"Power posing,* such as raising the arms above the head as when a player scores a touchdown, increases testosterone and decreases cortisol, the stress hormone. Contracted movements, on the other hand, diminish your personal power and, in turn, your effectiveness."

Remember this when you feel at your wit's end, down in the dumps, or ready to give up. Get out of your head and into your body as quickly as possible. Start observing your body, breathe, move, lift your arms up and wave your hands, open your chest really wide, shake that tail feather, and watch your mood shift almost instantly. Don't worry. Make an expansive move and be happy.

Eighty-four-years-young Tinney Davidson found herself alone and depressed after the death of her husband—until she began a movement ritual that boosted her mood.

Three times a day, Tinney opens her curtains wide and perches herself by her window near Highland Secondary School. Students walk by, and she waves her hands with tremendous enthusiasm. Schoolchildren wave back, and Tinney then smiles widely, rapidly patting her heart several times. These simple movements have become Tinney's sacrament. They boost her energy, lower her stress, and put her in a happy mood every morning. She feels so upbeat that she repeats her ritual at lunch break and again when school lets out. With her neighborly welcome waves, she not only reinforces the happy neural nets in her brain but also sparks new neurological connections in the schoolchildren. Some students who initially thought she was "weird" have come to count on her morning greeting. They say, "She pumps up everyone's attitude. When we see her waving and smiling, we wave and smile back. Everyone's mood is a little brighter." The students were so inspired by Tinney, they held a special assembly to express their gratitude.

BUST A MOVE

Let's pause for a moment to move in a way that feels expansive to you. Open your arms wide, or raise your hand in a high five, or mimic Steve Martin doing his "wild and crazy guy" shoulder shimmy. Sync that movement with your breathing and notice how that changes your mood. How did that feel? Do you notice a change in your thinking or energy level?

Consciously choose to pause and enjoy expansive moves as often as possible. It can create a big difference in how you feel, make decisions, or react to a situation. In Dr. Cuddy's words, "Change your mind and you change your behavior; change your behavior and you change your outcomes."

MOVEMENT ROCKS THE EMOTIONS

If you are ever confused about what emotions you are feeling and what might be influencing your thoughts and behavior, stop and observe your movements. Your brain, specifically your cerebrum, directs both your emotions and your movements. Movement awareness is a great sensor that can alert you when chronic, subconscious thinking patterns kick in. For example, you might notice that your whole body becomes tense when you try to take control of a situation you'd be better off letting go of. Or you might look down and see your leg shaking furiously, which could indicate that you are getting anxious or bored. These are the times to notice your movements and listen to what they are telling you. Then you can choose what to do next: Get up and move, stretch and expand your chest, take a breath and relax, or deliver that difficult communication you've been stuffing down.

One client had no idea he was broadcasting nervousness during TV interviews. Now he scans his body when in front of the camera, readily catches himself when he's nervous, sits back, and takes a deep breath. His interviews are more relaxed, and he doesn't distract the host and viewers by rocking back and forth.

The mind, emotions, and body form a close-knit, sophisticated system. Therefore, it makes sense that this added awareness serves as a doorway to our thinking and feelings.

It did for Leonard, a newly promoted vice president who called me to help him develop his *executive presence,* the corporate term for a person's ability to step into his or her new role when promoted. In WBI terms, executive presence is an embodied confidence everyone feels when a person walks into the room.

Sylvia Ann Hewlett, the founder of the NYC think tank the Center for Talent Innovation, interviewed 4,000 executives in August 2014. She told the *Wall Street Journal* that executive presence "is how you behave, how you speak, and how you look." The behavioral part, sometimes called gravitas, is most important, Hewlett said. In her book, *Executive Presence*: *The Missing Link between Merit and Success,* Hewlett writes: "Gravitas, first and foremost, is about confidence and staying calm in a stressful situation." When the executive who embodies this quality speaks, people listen. When he or she joins a team meeting, everyone pays attention, eager to hear where their leader is taking them next.

The problem is that even people who have performed 300 percent above their job objectives and showed leadership qualities to get promoted can still feel vulnerable when given more authority and responsibility. They don't step into their new role easily, and their body shows it.

This is what was happening to Leonard. Not long after he was promoted, his higher-ups reported a lack of leadership qualities. He couldn't look team members in the eye. His communication was unclear. His supervisors were unsure what to do. People in his department complained that his directives were difficult to decipher. Their comments included "He looks uncomfortable, lost, and out of place. He can't seem to communicate what he wants from us."

At my first meeting with Leonard, I noticed that his eyes were lowered the entire time we spoke. When I congratulated him on his promotion, his shoulders rose up and almost touched his ears. He also slid his chair back away from me. I knew that movement awareness would help Leonard understand what was blocking him from stepping into his leadership position.

I asked him to invite a few of his team members to participate in an exercise. My aim was to help him discover what was blocking his executive presence. Before his team arrived, I prompted Leonard to take deep breaths and notice any sensations in his body. He noticed that his breath was shallow, and his shoulders felt tense. He explained that his entire body felt like it was shrinking.

When his team walked into the room, I asked him to observe his body sensations again. He reported that his body had begun to shake. He also noticed that he was holding his breath. I encouraged him to stand in front of the room and face his team. I asked each person to acknowledge one quality they admired in Leonard. Each person offered a compliment, identifying one of Leonard's strengths. The group continued to praise Leonard. As they did, his shoulders rose closer and closer to his ears. Each time someone complimented him, he looked down at the floor and took a step backward. By the fifth accolade, he had backed up so far that he smacked into the wall behind him. He was a bit stunned and embarrassed. I thanked his team for participating and asked them to leave the room.

After they left I assisted Leonard to take a look at what the exercise and his body had shown him: that he was extremely uncomfortable receiving praise. For the next 15 minutes, I guided Leonard to observe what he felt while moving back and forth and looking down at the floor as I complimented him for his achievements. Emotions began to surface, and memories followed. Leonard recalled and shared an admonishment he'd heard from his father many times while growing up: "Don't get a big head and think you're better than everyone else." As a child, whenever he hit a home run or won an award, his father would warn him: "Don't get too big for your britches," then show Leonard the back of his hand.

Leonard discovered the link between his physical responses and his emotional state. "The only way I could avoid how I felt when my dad threatened me was by holding my breath, raising my shoulders, looking down, and backing away," he revealed. Leonard had pushed those memories out of his conscious mind until that afternoon. "I didn't even know that I was doing that with my staff," he said, surprised and yet relieved.

I invited the team back in and had Leonard share this new insight. The energy in the room was electric—everyone felt new respect for Leonard.

Over the next few weeks, Leonard stayed keenly aware of his body movements. He backed up less often and made direct eye contact with his staff. He began to accept his new leadership role and lost his fear of being hurt or seeming like a braggart. He is now an executive who stands tall, looks you in the eye, and leads with clarity and confidence.

TRIPPING OVER YOUR OWN TWO FEET

While Leonard's past challenges were in the boardroom, Roberta's were at center court during big tennis tournaments. "My coach and I have thought this through several times," she told me. "We can't figure out what's happening. I just lose control and start freezing and tripping over my feet during crucial points." With two important matches coming up in the next few days, she needed help.

Her mother had seen the PBS special *Heal Yourself: Mind over Medicine* and had received my *Whole Body Intelligence* DVD as a pledge gift. She called her daughter right away. "I think this guy can help you."

Roberta explained her dilemma to me: "Every time I win the first set, I have an anxiety attack and lose the next two sets." I asked her to shift her attention from her mind to her body, starting by observing her breath. She noticed her breath was short and labored, very high up in her chest. I explained that her shallow breathing pattern was a red flag. "When we sip our breath and don't breathe fully into the lungs," I explained, "we lock in our sympathetic nervous system, better known as fight-or-flight mode. On high alert, we behave as though danger awaits us."

She took a big gasp of air and fell silent. I had obviously touched a nerve. I waited for several seconds, then asked her to scan her body and tell me what she noticed. She reported tension in her chest, jaw, and shoulders. She was astonished to discover that her left hand was propelled forward and her right hand was pulled back. I instructed her to breathe deeply and allow her upper body, hands, and arms to move however they wanted. I also suggested she breathe into her belly and take a full deep breath. Like so many of us, she'd been trained to suck in her stomach. She told me she felt awkward as she breathed like this, as if her lower belly was foreign territory, but she followed my lead. I asked her to put 100 percent of her attention on both her hands and her arms, wait, and just observe until movement happened naturally.

After a few moments, Roberta had an urge to move her arms back and forth several times. A thought came to her: "It's as if part of me wants to move forward in my tennis career but part of me is petrified and holding back. The moment I got ranked as a professional and began playing bigger matches, something changed." Her arms and hands started moving back and forth even more as she said this. She continued to focus on her movements. She cried out, "It feels like I start to move forward but then I pull back, as if something bad will happen." I directed her to keep breathing and exaggerate her arm movements in both directions. She began crying. I asked what she was feeling and she replied, "Deep feelings of sadness are locked up in my chest, shoulders, and arms." After a few moments of observing these feelings, she nervously shared something she had buried years ago that had just come to the surface. "When I was 8, my dog, Rusty, died. He was my best friend. It was the worst time of my life. I held in all of my emotions by getting as small as I could." When I asked how she did that, she exclaimed, "By collapsing my chest and shoulders and rolling into a ball." Roberta shared that she hadn't wanted to burden anyone or show weakness, so she kept her emotions to herself. In her words, "I squeezed them all in."

Next we explored Roberta's experience of losing her dad in her early teens. Although she had been crumbling inside, she masked her grief because she didn't want to burden her mom. "She already had too much to deal with."

I asked her to check in with her body. She felt a familiar tension in her chest and shoulders, much like she'd experienced after the heart-wrenching loss of her dog and then her dad. I asked her to express what she had felt but never shared with her mom. Her answer took a few moments to surface. "I am afraid when things are going great that you will die and leave me, too."

I asked Roberta to repeat her statement several times while observing her body movements. As she did, her arms unlocked and rested at her sides while her chest and shoulders let go. She instantly felt a sense of calm pour over her. In a soft, clear voice, she said, "I've held that fear in most of my life. Every time my life was going great, I lost someone. Even being devoted to tennis cost me friends. The more I won, the more I had to practice, and I missed social events. The better I do, the more I lose people." I waited as years of emotion poured out of her body while she continued to breath, move, and express her feelings. Roberta's subconscious body-mind had confused winning with loss. It was time for her to rewire those neural nets.

I suggested she continue to breathe and feel into what she

had discovered in the session. I encouraged her to tell her mom what she had been holding in for a dozen years and literally get it off her chest and shoulders. I also suggested she send a text to any friends she has neglected and tell them how precious they are to her. She created a whole-body affirmation to run through her head and body during matches: "When I win and life goes well for me, people I love will stay in my life." She reported that her body loved it when she said this.

We talked the next day. She had a life-changing phone call with her mom that lifted enormous tension from her shoulders. She received wonderful supportive replies from close friends. And that afternoon she had her best practice session in weeks. "I ran around the court with ease and confidence," she said. We practiced her whole-body affirmation several times. She released even more tension from her body and said she couldn't wait to get back on the court.

Days later Roberta won the next two tournaments and had this to say: "When I won the first set of each match, the anxiety returned. Instead of freezing and trying to will it away, I located the anxiety in my body, started moving and shaking those areas free, and recited my new affirmation. I quickly recovered and relaxed each time. Tennis became fun again." Roberta won all three sets both days.

This example demonstrates how we can turn any situation around with movement awareness. When Roberta starts to spiral down, she now knows to use movement awareness to tip her off to the thoughts and beliefs that undermine her game. This changes her state and, in turn, her chances of winning on the court and in the rest of her life.

Whether on the tennis court, at the office, or back home after a long day, we can choose to observe our movements, to notice our thoughts and the messages we send out with our body. You can improve your presentation and response to others by expanding your awareness in this way. What's more, others' responses to you will change.

Continue observing your movements with awareness as a new tool to help you "catch the beat," access your deepest truth in an efficient way, and move in the right direction.

In the next chapter, you will get to explore some of your own movement patterns and memories through self-assessment exercises and a process I call your *movement autobiography*.

CHAPTER 4

YOUR MOVEMENT AUTOBIOGRAPHY

*There's no biography so interesting as the one
in which the biographer is present.*

—ORSON WELLES

MOVEMENT AWARENESS COMBINED WITH an investigation into your history allows you to dive deep into unconscious aspects of yourself. I've purposely revisited many earlier times of my life to uncover blind spots and close the gap between my desired behaviors and habitual responses that worked against me.

For example, at times when I walked onstage to give a lecture or talk, my body would betray me. I was always excited and confident and made sure I was well prepared. But the moment my feet hit the stage, it was a different story. First I'd feel a grip in my belly. Then my face would get hot and beads of sweat would roll down my chest. I was perplexed. This went on for several months until a colleague said, "You need to go back into your history and find out why your body acts up when you go onstage."

I started that process by sitting down with a notebook and making a list of all the times I had been on a public stage. I visualized each one. First on my list was the time I acted in a school play in elementary school. Then I saw myself at my Bar Mitzvah, standing before a congregation of 200 leading the Sabbath prayers. After the prayer services, I was required to give a thank-you speech. In the 10th grade, I addressed 100 parents at a banquet for my high school fraternity. Nothing. Nada. My body had nothing to say to me about those appearances. I continued writing, taking this trip down memory lane, and there he was. The memory was as vivid as could be: Mr. Donaldson, our 12th grade chorus teacher, his conductor's baton in his hand. Now my body was talking—the familiar grip, the heat in my face, the beads of sweat rolling down my chest. With clear intent to unpack the experience, I decided to consciously regress to my interaction onstage with Mr. Donaldson.

In the psychological context, *regression* means revisiting, even reenacting, events from the past. By reliving high-impact experiences, we can see the untoward influence they have on current behavior. In the context of Whole Body Intelligence (WBI), this happens in the body.

So I allowed myself to engage with what was occurring in my body rather than resist or judge my reaction. It was as if I'd stepped into a time machine. I was right there, a self-conscious 12th grader, standing onstage among the school chorus, singing "This Land Is Mine" from *Exodus* in front of the entire student body. Then my body jolted. I heard Mr. Donaldson yell, "Stop!" My whole body shook as the memory poured in.

Mr. Donaldson had caught me giggling at the end of the front row, stage left. The sight of him waving his arms just cracked me up. I was trying to control it when he ordered the chorus to stop and pointed his baton directly at me. "You!" he shouted. "Off the stage!" Like a turtle pulling into his shell, I disappeared into a corner for protection. I felt a wave of shame. I was horrified that everyone had seen me disgraced in that way. The entire school had witnessed my humiliation. What's more, my moment of shame was forever inscribed in the yearbook. Even at our 10-year reunion, my classmates were still laughing about that day.

Revisiting high-impact events such as my exodus from the stage can lead to revealing discoveries. We touch the experience that influenced our view of the world and who we are in it. We recognize the effect it had—and still has—on our responses to life events. We activate Whole Body Intelligence, assume body movements and postures associated with a particular experience, and uncover unconscious imprints that shape our thinking, emotional reaction, and behavior.

Daniel Cassanto, PhD, of the Max Planck Institute for Psycholinguistics and Katinka Dijkstra of Erasmus University explored this in an April 2010 study. They concluded, "Bodily movements can influence the rate at which autobiographical memories are recalled as well as the emotional content of the memories." Dr. Cassanto and Dijkstra led 24 undergraduates through movement exercises while posing open-ended statements such as "Tell me about a time when you felt proud of yourself" or "Tell me about a time you felt ashamed." They reported: "Participants' bodily movements influenced the recollection of emotional memories. Processes like movement awareness activate the same systems in the brain associated with the original experiences."

This is how the *movement autobiography* process can help you close the gap. You will see and feel the link between how your body reacted then and how you react to similar events now. This process is like having a periscope—a tool that provides a view of that which is ordinarily out of your direct line of sight. This expanded awareness provides you with the opportunity for a do-over—what dictionary.com defines as "a second chance." A do-over is more than a retraction or apology; it is an opportunity to change your brain. You respond in a way that is congruent with who you are here and now rather than respond blindly to unresolved hurts from the past. A do-over is the first step toward creating a new neural pathway. This is how human beings change.

Here is an example of how this plays out. Not long after reliving the *Exodus* incident, I traveled to Scottsdale, Arizona, to conduct a training session for a group of about 75 event planners. As usual I arrived well over an hour early to survey the room. As soon as I walked onstage, the sweat started rolling down my chest. I observed my body and let it speak. I felt every part of me begin to contract as my subliminal fear of getting kicked off the stage activated. Clearly, my high school *Exodus* lived on in my body. However, I was now aware of the real source of the clammy, sweaty, heart-racing reaction. I wasn't anxious about standing in front of a group of event planners; my body was reacting to a setting that was similar to a setting where I'd felt humiliated in the past.

I had 60 minutes until the group arrived. I decided to use body movements to activate the systems in my brain associated with my *Exodus*. First I allowed myself to fully feel the familiar contraction, then I exaggerated it by ducking behind the stage, pulling into my shell, and cowering in a corner. That mortified 17-year-old rushed into my awareness. The fear started to build. Here was the key. Rather than cower like I did in high school, I had a chance for a do-over. I opened my arms wide, shook my body, and assumed a power pose. I waved my arms and imagined shouting at Mr. Donaldson for tossing me off the stage. In a matter of moments, that short movement regression and do-over exercise dissolved the old emotions and bodily responses that had been activated. This allowed me to walk onstage in full possession of myself rather than lost in a reaction rooted in the past.

I shared this *Exodus* and do-over experience in a keynote address for the CEO Club held at the Marriott Baltimore Harborplace Hotel. After the talk a CEO of a large corporation came up to me and said, "I feel stagnant in my body and stuck in my life. I always feel like something is holding me back."

David continued by telling me he was uncomfortable in his body from putting on an extra 40 pounds over the past year. To me I only saw a bright-eyed man with a huge heart that shined through his eyes, so I was quite surprised by what he said next. "My wife often calls me her 'grumpy husband.' My kids dubbed me 'Crabby Daddy.' Even my leadership team says I'm rougher around the edges then I used to be."

After hearing my *Exodus* story, he wanted to revisit some of his past experiences to help him find the causes of his change in attitude and his body.

He arrived in my California office. David was happy to be on the West Coast. "All I do is sit: 2 hours a day in my car, 16 at my desk, then at night I sit on my sofa and watch TV until I go to bed," he explained. "It's so nice to be out here in nature with you."

I sensed he needed to get outside and move his body, so I suggested we begin our weekend by going for a hike.

We drove to the base of Mount Tamalpais. Standing on the fire road at the trailhead, I explained that we would begin his session with body awareness exercises and directed him to connect with his body as he took a few full breaths, breathing in through his nose and out through his mouth. Next I suggested he observe the quality of his breathing. This was a novel idea for David, but he nodded his head and gave it a whirl, taking his first step toward connecting his thoughts and his body.

David began to feel his emotions rise. He started to hold his breath. His body became tense. I waited a few moments until David recognized what was happening in his body. I instructed him to open his eyes and continue to observe his breathing and his body as we began to walk. He froze, saying, "I don't want to move." I asked if this feeling was familiar. Did it remind him of any particular time in his past? He nodded yes. I invited him to close his eyes, continue to observe the feeling, and see what his body wanted to say. I asked him to repeat the phrase "I don't want to move" several times and instructed him to pay close attention to how his body responded. By the fifth repetition, David noted that he was seething with anger: "I feel a massive, boiling ball of rage shaking my insides."

After a few moments, I asked, "What do you see?"

"I can see myself at age 18," he replied. "I'm at a track meet. I just finished running the 100-yard dash."

As if it were yesterday, David saw himself cross the finish line. He'd finished in third place. "Not bad," he thought. Both of the guys who'd beat him were state champions. He looked up into the bleachers, searching for his father. David's fist was raised in triumph. When he saw the look on his father's face, his fist dropped to his side. He stood transfixed, watching his father shake his head from side to side.

On the drive home, his father said, "Son, I'm really disappointed in you. You had those guys beat at about 80 yards, and you blew it. You should've won that race."

David remembered sitting in the passenger seat of his dad's car, staring at the Oldsmobile symbol on the glove box. He'd been taught never to question or talk back to his dad. He didn't dare say that the guys who'd come in first and second were seasoned champions. Or that he'd run his personal-best time yet in the 100-yard dash.

David told me how much he had loved running before the painful confusion of that day. As he spoke about that afternoon, I saw his body recoil as if his father's disapproval were happening in the here and now. He held his breath and collapsed into his chest. "I feel numb," he said. "At the end of the season, my coach told me I had great potential, but I quit track and never went out for sports or took an exercise class again."

David had an aha moment when he realized how much impact that incident had on how he relates to himself and others. Whether with his wife, his kids, or his staff, he had a tendency to scan faces for any inkling of disapproval. If he found a whisper of disfavor, his default, knee-jerk response was to shut down his body and freeze. This was David's defense mechanism, a way to find protection from the storm of feelings that came with disappointing someone he cares about. Now that David had a cognitive understanding coupled with a conscious experience of his unconscious physical response to disapproval, he was primed for the next step. He was ready for a do-over.

I guided David to not curtail any urges he was experiencing in his body and encouraged him to say whatever he didn't get to say after that track meet. "You can rewrite that part of your history right now," I explained. "Let your body do whatever it didn't get to do back then."

David closed his eyes and listened to his body for several moments. He shook his shoulders and legs. A few moments later, he began to whisper what he'd wanted to say to his father. "Stop pressuring me!" he said under his breath. He could barely access the words, having kept his feelings down for 30 years.

I encouraged David to run about 20 yards and then turn around and come back. He ran 30, then turned around. Halfway back he stopped, put his hands on his thighs, then stood up and shouted, "Nothing I do is good enough for you."

I told him to run harder and yell even louder. He ran full blast, shouting, "Stop pressuring me!" For several minutes he stomped around saying everything he'd wanted to say to his dad. His whole body opened up. When he was finished shouting, he stood before me like a proud peacock. He smiled and opened his arms wide in triumph. "I've been holding that in since I was a teenager." As we reflected further, David recognized how repressing his feelings had affected his communication style as well as his relationship with his body. He had directed his frustration and anger at many, many people over the years. He'd even taken it out on his own body by not getting any exercise. "I am always pushing to prove myself, and avoiding my body in the process."

David had a significant breakthrough that day. He unearthed an unconscious belief that had kept him from living an active life. His unresolved feelings had caused him to repress his natural athletic self and become sedentary. He reported, "Wow, now I can feel the way I've been holding myself back; this belief literally immobilized me."

I encouraged David to speak aloud the specific belief that his body had held below the level of conscious awareness. He whispered, "When I move my body, I will be humiliated. No way am I going to risk disapproval." I encouraged him to say just the first line even louder and let his body do whatever it wanted, what it couldn't do many years ago. He said the words, "When I move my body, I will be humiliated." He said this several times. With each repetition his legs shook as his energy began to build. Then he began walking slowly along the trail. He kept saying this over and over and louder and louder while his pace became faster and faster. After several minutes he broke into a run. I was reminded of the moment in the movie *Forrest Gump* when Jenny yelled, "Run, Forrest, run," and Forrest's leg braces broke off. David had a different kind of braces that he shed as he headed for the top of the mountain.

He ran with his chest high, clearly enjoying himself. He took in the mountain and scenery below, laughing and raising his arms in triumph. In that moment I was in awe of David's desire and commitment to transform his life. Even more impressive was how courageous he was throughout the process.

I joined him on the mountaintop and we formulated a new belief to anchor in his body: "I am an athlete, and moving my body brings happiness and approval." Movement awareness, regressing to his history, and having a do-over started David on a path of healing. He began jogging at lunchtime with his staff and dropped 40 pounds. Within months he was training for a marathon. He planned outdoor activities and fun vacations with his family.

WRITING YOUR MOVEMENT AUTOBIOGRAPHY

Like David, we all have signature movement patterns, gestures, and facial expressions that lock us up. In subsequent sessions David continued to learn about his past by writing his movement history down on paper. He found that many of his signature moves had repeated throughout his life. Some protected him from criticism. Others were learned from simply being around his parents and subconsciously mimicking their movement patterns. When David recognized that his walk was almost an exact replica of his father's, he was surprised, even shocked.

The tendency to copy our parents' walk is so subtle we barely notice it. Watch a young boy walking next to his father and you will see this subconscious copycat effect.

Lisa Nalven, MD, a behavioral pediatrician at the Kireker Center for Child Development in New Jersey, explains, "Mimicry begins at birth—many newborns, for instance, copy facial movements such as sticking out their tongue." These are the types of signature movements you may unearth while doing your movement autobiography.

Rachel Ruiz, a third-year Vanderbilt University School of Medicine student, was shocked to learn just how much a parent's level of activity versus sedentary behavior influences their children. Her work with children confirms that they mimic their parents.

We know that children develop their perceptions of themselves, others, and the world around them during their early years. Science has confirmed this with brain wave scanning, which shows that kids are primarily in a beta state for their first 6 years. Beta is a highly suggestible state of mind that allows myriad impressions, many of them nonverbal, to enter our nervous system and form our sense of self.

The Apple Never Falls Far from the Tree

This proverb that originated in the East is frequently used to highlight the way children take on the characteristics of their family. I saw a vivid example of this in a photo of a child at an NFL game. A boy of no more than 6 years of age had his middle finger sticking up and a scary scowl on his face. Where would a young child learn to yell, display so much anger, and give the finger? He was clearly mimicking someone else. A child hears and sees his dad use a derogatory name with an accompanying gesture. Then his dad's friend gives him a high five. The boy has just seen adults reward one another for that behavior. And these aren't just any adults; these are the adults he naturally looks up to at his age. So what does he turn around and do? Exactly what his father has shown him men do.

This scenario is illustrated in the movie *42*, which captures the struggles and triumphs of Branch Rickey and Jackie Robinson. Rickey, the owner of the Brooklyn Dodgers, signed Jackie Robinson, breaking the color barrier in Major League Baseball. In a riveting scene, we see a young boy at his very first baseball game. He is thrilled as he waits for his favorite player and hero, Pee Wee Reese, to show up on the field. When Pee Wee runs out of the dugout with his team, the kid is ecstatic. But when Pee Wee's teammate Jackie Robinson runs onto the field, his dad raises his fist, brings his hands to his mouth like a megaphone, and screams, "Nigger, we don't want you here." The kid looks around, confused. Many of the adults are doing exactly as his dad. He raises his fist, forms his hands into a megaphone, and shouts "We don't want you here" at Jackie. He looks around to his dad and the men sitting near him for approval. Then his idol, Pee Wee Reese, walks from shortstop to first base, puts his arm around Jackie, and stares at the fans. The kid bows his head and sinks down to hide in his third-row seat. Even though he feels ashamed in that moment, he is likely to mimic his dad in the future by shouting obscenities through his hand megaphone.

Most of us start copying our parents at a very young age. As we get older, we copy heroes we see on TV or the cool kids at school. Evolution designed us to do this—to absorb the norms of our tribe. That process begins and is the strongest at home.

I designed a specific movement exercise to address this in WBI workshops. Participants are led through movement and visualization exercises that allow them to see and feel themselves as a child, as a teen, and as an adult, moving through key life events. Although they may not have a conscious memory associated with these events, tuning in to their body's reactions as they visualize and move often helps them discover the source of signature moves they display today. Even where conscious memory—visual, auditory, kinesthetic—is scant or nonexistent, the body *was* there every moment of your life. And the body holds a record of everything.

I invite you to do the following exercise and begin to write, and eventually rewrite, your movement autobiography.

The People You Mimic the Most: Your Mom and Dad

Bring to mind the primary person who took care of you— Mom, Dad, Grandma—when you were small. If you never met your parents and were raised by relatives or in foster care, choose the person who influenced you the most before age 6.

Take a moment and, in your mind's eye, visualize how your mom moves or moved through life. Take a deep breath in and out as you do this, then open your eyes.

Mimic any gestures you recall your mom making. She may have swung her hands, scrunched her nose, or exhaled with a puff when she was frustrated. As you do this, notice what sensations and emotions you feel.

Write down anything you have discovered.

Next get up and walk the way you remember your mom walked. After you walk like her, take a moment to pause and reflect. Scan your body and observe. You are beginning to piece together your movement history. The aim of this exercise is to discover unconscious movement patterns so you can change them and get better results.

Take a deep breath in and out before we continue.

Now let's explore your dad's signature moves.

Take a moment and, in your mind's eye, visualize how your dad moves or moved through life. Take a deep breath in and out as you do this, then open your eyes and return to the page.

What's the first thing you saw? Notice any body reactions that you are having from seeing him move. Take a deep breath in and out. Mimic any gestures you recall your dad making: his smile or frown, posture, hand movements, etc. As you do this, notice any sensations or emotions.

What have you discovered?

Now get up and walk the way you saw your dad walk.

Take a few deep breaths in and out. After you walk like your dad, take a moment to pause and reflect. Scan your body and observe.

To help you capture important observations, fill in the blanks below and notice any body responses you have as you write.

I notice the following sensations, emotions, and discoveries when I take on the movements of my mother: _____

_____

I notice the following sensations, emotions, and discoveries when I take on the movements of my father: _____

_____

Which of the above discoveries are still present in the way you move through life today? _____

_____

What movement patterns or traits did you learn from your parents that you want to stay aware of and change? _____

_____

"OUT OF THIS WORLD"

Sarah had a valuable insight when she did this exercise in a WBI workshop. She visualized how her mom moved as we began the exercise. Her mom was in a familiar, frenzied state—her signature "wait for no one" dash. Sarah also noticed that this mad-dash movement had a flavor of tentativeness.

"At the age of 90, my mother is still in a constant frenzy, although now she does her mad dash with a walker," Sarah shared. "Whether she's bringing a meal for a friend or heading downstairs to play bingo, she's in go-go-go mode from sunup to sundown until she finally plotzes down on the sofa. She is the kind of person who starts packing for a vacation a week ahead of time and arrives at the airport 3 hours early. I have walked into many restaurants with my mother a full 30 minutes before our reservation."

Sarah explained that her mom was a caring person, but her

"racehorse with blinders" movements often resulted in her not hearing what other people were saying. "She has three signature retorts for just about everything," Sarah said. "Whether family, food, her favorite baseball team, or the latest news report, her response is either 'Out of this world,' 'Not bad,' or 'Lousy.'"

I continued the exercise, directing the workshop group to move about the room and talk to other participants while mimicking their parents.

Sarah walked around the room mimicking her mom in that got-to-get-there-now mode. She felt empathetic toward her mom and yet very disconnected from her own body. She also felt distant from the participants she spoke with in the exercise. Her conversations went like this:

Participant: "How are you doing?"

Sarah, at random: "Not bad," "Lousy," or "Out of this world."

She felt more and more unstable as she moved about the room. People were having odd reactions to her. She mostly saw looks of bewilderment on their faces.

On the other hand, when she walked like her dad, she felt laid back and introverted. "He always walked with his eyes lowered," she said. "We often joked that if anyone dropped money on the ground, Dad would surely find it." She walked around the room like her dad, shaking hands with other participants but never looking up. "I felt sadness in my heart and nervousness in my belly," she shared. "I could feel his big heart but also his shyness and past hurts that had him not look people in the eye."

This exercise helped Sarah see the bigger picture of her life and clued her in to the many gestures and movement patterns she had adopted from her parents. When she caught herself looking down while speaking to someone at the workshop, she caught the movement, lifted her head, and felt more present and engaged.

Months later Sarah wrote me, saying, "This added perspective made all the difference in my ability to respond to unexpected curveballs that life throws at me."

This exercise helped a 34-year-old saleswoman who was also on go-go-go mode wherever she went. Tina came to a WBI workshop desperate to change this pattern. She had become aware of the tremendous stress it put on her body as well as her relationships both at work and in her personal life. She simply had to arrive for any appointment ridiculously early, sometimes hours ahead. She would struggle to sit through team meetings even though she loved her team. She even found it difficult to take pleasure in seeing a movie or having a meal with a friend.

When Tina tapped into her mom's way of moving through life, she saw her mom drunk, staggering around the house. As Tina started to imitate her mom's movements, emotions began to surface and specific memories appeared. Her mom was always late, whether picking Tina up after school or going to church on Sunday. Tina's most vivid memories were of events that had occurred on Sundays. Her dad would leave the house early to attend his men's meeting at church. He always saved two seats: one for her and one for her mother. Every Sunday morning, Tina's mom would race around the house, still hung over from the night before, doing everything but getting dressed for church. She wouldn't dress Tina, either. By the time they left the house, the service had already started. Every Sunday Tina would squirm as she took her seat next to her dad. He'd pinch her hard and give her an angry look. Once they got home after church, he would yell at Tina and her mom. Sometimes he became physically abusive.

In front of a roomful of workshop participants, Tina shouted, "No wonder I am petrified of being late." She recognized the feeling she'd had as a girl, moving frantically, off balance like her mom, squishing her body tight, bracing herself for Dad's painful pinch. She shared with the group that this is how she moves through life on a daily basis, especially if she has to meet someone. "Even if I'm just meeting a friend for a cup of tea, I feel totally on edge. And that edginess doesn't go away once I arrive." This awareness allowed Tina to find ways of slowing down. She adopted a whole new movement pattern. This initially took a great deal of intentional focus, but in time her slowed-down way of moving about her world became second nature. What's more, changing her movement patterns helped her change the subconscious belief that she needed to rush and be hours early or she would get scolded and, possibly, hurt. As the workshop continued, Tina became even more aware that she was squirming in her seat, hoping to be invisible. She readily linked this with her body's fear when she would inch toward her dad in the church pew. On workshop breaks she practiced moving more gently instead of racing around fearing she might be late when the break was over.

Tina liberated herself from her overamped go-go-go mode through movement awareness. She continues to rewrite her movement autobiography by showing up on time, not hours early, and in a much more relaxed and present state.

You too can rewrite your movement autobiography by tuning in to signature moves you learned and adopted when you were small.

NOT ALL MOVES WE ADOPT ARE DETRIMENTAL

Identifying our patterns gives us the choice to use them or change them. For example, my first year in junior high coincided with the first year of desegregation in Baltimore. I was bused into a neighborhood that was primarily composed of African Americans and Latinos. I became friends with kids from many cultures I had not been exposed to before. My new friends were so cool—the way they dressed, the way they moved with a swagger. They possessed such a light, humorous attitude. I mimicked their gestures and found myself starting to walk with a similar swagger and cool stride. To this day that strut is in my muscle memory. At times I strut intentionally when it suits a situation.

Here's another example. After college I spent many years studying yoga, meditation, and other teachings in India, Japan, and Hawaii. People from those cultures often bow with their palms together in greeting or to say thank-you. I adopted this gesture and often, without thinking about it, bow when greeting someone. My body memory stored those movements and gestures and sewed them into the fabric of who I am. And it always feels good when I do it.

On the other hand, some of our movements don't feel good at all. As a young kid, my cousins and I left our neighborhood one day. It was the first time we'd wandered beyond Lower Park Heights in northwest Baltimore. We got beat up by some rough guys. This happened more than once. After that experience I took on cautious movements and a shrinking posture to protect myself.

The point is this: Movement awareness allows you to make choices, to keep what feels authentic and empowering, and to let go of what doesn't.

TUNE IN TO YOUR MOVEMENT HISTORY EVEN MORE

We all have initiatory moments in our lives that influence how we move. For David it was a track meet. For Roberta, the tennis pro you met in Chapter 3, it was watching someone close to her die.

As you access certain memories, observe what happens in your body. Take a moment to focus on any sensations that occur and notice if images or body memories arise. Feel free to move and make sounds or do whatever your body wants to do as you contemplate each event. Then write down what you have noticed.

For instance, how did you feel when you entered preschool or spent time away from your family for the first time? Did you walk in happy and eager, or were you shy and more comfortable staying in the corner? How did you walk up to the front of the room when it was time for show-and-tell? As a child, how did you walk into your first visit to a dentist or doctor? What happened in your body when you knew you were having a shot or vaccination?

How was your first date or your first boy-girl dance? Did you freeze, become a wallflower, or get down and twist and shout?

Did you ever lose a job or have a business failure that still affects how you move?

Take your time to reflect on other high-impact, marker moments in your life and how you moved in those situations. Write down what you've discerned and continue to bring awareness to your body's reactions.

For instance, in my movement autobiography, I became aware of how I mimicked my mom's fear of heights. Every Saturday when I was a kid, my mom and I would go to Hutzler's department store and ride the escalator up to the second-floor restaurant for lunch. She would hold her breath and cringe the minute we got on the escalator. I wasn't aware of it, but I followed her lead and held my breath too. Likewise, whenever we would drive over the Delaware Memorial Bridge to Atlantic City, she would tell me not to look. The tendency to hold my breath and cringe still grabs me whenever I climb a ladder. When I would climb up to go down a waterslide, I felt the fear. I even experienced it when I was atop the imitation Eiffel Tower at the Paris Las Vegas Hotel. There were protective railings on the waterslide and a screen protecting me from falling off the faux Eiffel; nonetheless, my tendency to cringe and hold my breath would kick in. Once I became aware of this pattern, I was able to catch it and intentionally relax. Just becoming aware is not enough, however: We have to consciously work at changing hand-me-down movements we picked up from our parents.

USING YOUR MOVEMENT HISTORY TO YOUR ADVANTAGE

Jim Carrey, the genius body-centered actor, is very in touch with his body movements as well as his movement history. He is an example of someone who uses history to his advantage: He consciously imitates his dad's movements in each of his films. In the November 2013 issue of *Energy Times*, he shared that he gives a shout-out to his father in each film by integrating his dad's mannerisms, traits, and movements into the physical character of every part he plays. Carrey says that he embodied and exaggerated his dad's movement patterns in *The Truman Show*, and Carrey came across as real largely because he was consciously moving with awareness. Like many actors, speakers, and performers, he accesses his movement history to enrich his performance. It helps him get into character, entertain others, or illustrate a point.

Next time you are in a high-stakes situation—a sales call or lunch with a dream date—tune in to your inner voice and ask, "How am I moving through this moment?" Listen to what your body is telling you. Use movement awareness to your advantage.

You have now raised your awareness, discovered more about *you*, and learned to observe and change your breath, body, and movement patterns.

You are now ready and equipped for the next chapter, where you will become Jedi-like to conquer one of the biggest buzzkills in life: chronic stress.

PART II

DESTRESS ON DEMAND

CHAPTER 5

STRESS: IT'S NOT ALL IN YOUR HEAD

PUERTO VALLARTA, MEXICO, 1989. I was headed to Yelapa, Mexico, for a week to train a group of somatic therapists from California. We'd had a smooth flight from San Francisco to Puerto Vallarta. After a delicious lunch on the beach in PV, our host approached the table and informed us that our fishing boat to Yelapa was ready. There are no roads from Puerto Vallarta to Yelapa.

The boat ride across Bahía de Banderas, the seventh largest bay in the world, took 45 minutes. We pulled into the southernmost cove, surrounded by the mountainous jungle of the Sierra Madre Occidental. The village of Yelapa features steep hills and winding paths up and up the mountain and into the jungle. We weren't surprised to learn that there were no street names, no maps, and no electricity except at one local café and club called the Yacht. There was only one phone in the village.

We were led up a path to the casita (a small house) where the training was to take place. Three local women came in with tortillas and pies they had made in an outdoor clay oven.

The smell of jungle mixed with the fragrance of fresh-baked goods was intoxicating.

After eating one of the best slices of pie ever, I asked to be shown to my room so I could get a good night's rest and prepare for the morning session. The organizers of the training had arranged for me to have my own private *palapa,* away from the rest of the group. I thought to myself, "My own *palapa.* Oh, I'm going to sleep well tonight." Moments later a guide arrived, pointed up the hill, and said, "*Ven conmigo*" (Come with me). He handed me a headlamp for coming up and down the trail at night, and warned: "Amigo, we have a lot of centipedes and scorpions around here, so turn your shoes upside down and shake them out before you put them on." I felt my stomach drop and my heart rate jump. "What will happen if I get bit by a scorpion?" I asked. His answer was nonchalant. "We will need to take you by boat for the antidote."

We continued up a steep dirt path deep into the jungle. My guide carried my suitcase with effortless grace until he stopped and placed it on the dirt path. I asked, "Why are we stopping?" He replied, "Amigo, this is your *palapa,*" and pointed to an open-sided dwelling with a thatched roof made of dried palm leaves. No walls. No door. Just a hammock with a large bug net over it.

He left me alone, high up in the jungle with a single candle. I immediately climbed into the netted hammock, closed my eyes, and took some deep relaxing breaths in and let out some big sighs to calm me. The bugs must have heard the call, as they appeared quickly in large colonies, buzzing around the covered hammock. Darkness came quickly. I laid there, listening to the strange sounds of the jungle—snorts and squeals, a variety of animal languages, critters moving about in the dirt beneath my hammock—and repeatedly pushing the image of a scorpion out of my mind. I did not sleep much that night.

With the early-morning light came new sounds: the staccato knock-knock-knock of woodpeckers, the cooing of doves, loud calls and trill songs of exotic birds. I looked over the edge of my hammock to see a multicolored parrot in a nearby tree checking me out. I looked at my watch; it was time to head down the hill and join the group for breakfast at the casita. I brushed my teeth with bottled water and shook my shoes to evict any scorpions that thought they'd found a new home. All clear, I got dressed and off I went.

Once again the local women brought us a wonderful meal. We ate plates full of homemade cornbread and tropical fruits, then began the training.

I started by asking everyone to tune in to their intentions for the week and share them with the group. Some wanted to gain greater understanding of how they could use breathing and body-centered tools with their clients. Others saw the week as an opportunity to do some work on themselves—to uncover and change the habits and patterns blocking the happiness, success, and enriched relationships they desired. Everyone was also looking forward to a week without electricity and cars.

Next I directed the group to stand up and start moving around the room while stating their intentions out loud several times. Almost immediately one student became emotional. Tears filled her eyes as she felt how sad she was around her unfulfilled dreams when she said them out loud. Others began to get in touch with feelings in their bodies around their own intentions. I instructed the group to allow themselves to unwind any feelings that wanted to surface. I advised them to follow their movements, make sounds—do whatever their bodies wanted to do—to express whatever they were feeling in their bodies in a bigger way. "Let it all come out," I shouted. "Express whatever your body is telling you as you declare your desires."

They started to pop like popcorn, one at a time. Some were flailing their arms, several were shouting things like "Why did you tell me I couldn't do it? I needed you and you weren't there for me!" One woman let out a shrill so loud that even the birds stopped singing for a moment. Kernels were definitely popping.

A few minutes later, I heard footsteps running up to our casita. Several villagers had become concerned when they heard the scream that exploded out of that woman's body. I attempted to explain, speaking to the man who spoke fluent English. "We are moving stress out of our bodies through breathing, moving, and expressing what we feel. Many of us carry stress from events in our past and from thinking about our future. We are getting it out of our bodies this week." The villagers looked stumped, shrugged their shoulders, and glanced at each other in wonder. The English-speaking man explained, "They don't know what you mean by 'stress' or how it lives in your body. We have no concept or word for that here."

They were confounded. They knew the pain of a scorpion

bite. They knew the grief of suddenly losing a family member. They didn't understand how a person could hold on to it and still be affected by it years later.

While living among the people of Yelapa over the next week, I saw why they had no word for stress. They did not wake up when the alarm told them to get out of bed; they rose with the roosters and started moving their bodies straight away. They didn't sit, like many of us today do. No desks, no computers or smartphones to start the first few hours of the day. When I walked down the path to the casita each morning, I saw men, women, kids, and elders—all of them busy and happy. Villagers swept the porch, rolled masa for tortillas, sliced vegetables for stew, and stirred big pots of beans. Men and boys went out in the bay to catch fish and cleaned them when they returned to the dock. Barefoot children played and tended the gardens while others carried bags of rice to their houses. Everyone was engaged in physical activity. Everywhere I went, the locals smiled and waved. No one complained, and I didn't see or hear so much as a single argument between people all week. Nor did I see anyone frown or get lost and frozen in thought.

In the evenings family members would gather, light candles, and eat dinner together. They told stories, sang, and laughed until the candles went out. Kids, elders, moms, and dads—they all worked, played, and ate together. No one was alone and no one looked worried or depressed. From what I witnessed, they never got stuck in the mind or spent time thinking about the past or future.

These people were proof that humans could live in the

moment and, as Ram Dass put it, "be here now," free of mental stress, worrisome thoughts about the future, or residual
trauma from the past. These people knew little else than the
moment they were living in. No wonder the concept of carrying stress in the body was foreign. I was witnessing the closest
example I had ever seen of what we now call a Blue Zone.

The term *Blue Zone* was coined by researchers Gianni Pes,
MD, Michel Poulain, PhD, and Anne Herm, MD, while conducting a study for the Vienna Institute of Demography and
the Austrian Academy of Sciences that was ultimately published in the *Vienna Yearbook of Population Research*. The
study's aim was to compare the characteristics of four geo-
graphic areas with an unusually high percentage of centenarians. They looked at the population of Ogliastra in Sardinia,
Okinawa in Japan, the Nicoya peninsula in Costa Rica, and
the island of Ikaria in Greece. They zeroed in on the villages
with the highest longevity and drew concentric blue circles on
the map. The areas inside those circles were referred to as the
Blue Zone. These were geographically isolated populations
either on islands or in the mountains. The residents in these
areas maintained a simple lifestyle that involved hours of physical activity. People had little, if any, ongoing stress and plenty
of unquestioned support from family and the community.

Blue Zone was popularized by explorer and author Dan
Buettner in his 2010 book, *The Blue Zones: Lessons for Living
Longer from the People Who've Lived the Longest*. Buettner
and other researchers identified traits these populations exhibit
in common: a healthy, plant-based diet and constant physical
activity that is an integral part of daily life. These peoples also

have a sense of purpose, and every age group is socially active and engaged with their communities.

I don't know the average life span of the Yalapans, and I know they are 45 minutes from a popular tourist area, but from what I witnessed back then, they were certainly living a Blue Zone lifestyle. In WBI terms, they lived body first.

Most of us in the postindustrial, technology-dominated world, however, do not live in a Blue Zone, nor do we live that lifestyle. The good news is that we don't need to move to a remote village to model a body-first lifestyle. We can bring about a fundamental change in our worldview and life by being Whole Body Intelligent. Your next step in the journey toward that goal is to understand the physiological effects of stress on your body, where it lives within you, and the role it plays in your life now.

OVERUSING OUR BUILT-IN STRESS RESPONSE

Unlike Blue Zone people, whose lives are governed by their internal clock and body rhythms, we in the high-tech world tend to live by external clocks, calendars, and deadlines. The pace of life in a world dominated by technology is accelerated. We are engaged in stressful activities and exposed to stress-producing elements in our environment at all hours of the day and night. For many of us, life is an ongoing 911 situation with impossibly long task lists and daily situations that cause us to overreact as if we are faced with a physical threat. You may get the news that your company is downsizing, or your teenager has failed his physics test, and you react as though your car has skidded out of control and is directly in the path of an oncoming vehicle. You might react to each of these circumstances with a high-amplitude stress response similar to that of early humans being chased by a predator. Our innate fight-or-flight mechanism is designed for use in times of serious danger, but we often perceive danger when the threat isn't imminent or life threatening. Unfortunately the body can't always tell the difference between what's real and what's fabricated, so our stress response gets overused. Our stress switch may even flip to a permanent "on" position.

The reason for this is simple: The stress response is hard-wired to survival instincts, which kick in when we feel afraid. Fear signals the fight-or-flight response to engage. This happens lightning fast, before the executive function of the neo-cortex can intervene. We need fear to warn us when danger is lurking; however, if our stress switch is on most or all of the time, this can damage our health, negatively impact performance, and foster relationship problems. Our stress hormones are designed to help us, but when they are overproduced in the body or not turned off once the threat has passed, they promote cellular damage and accelerate aging. An excess of stress hormones can contribute to anxiety, depression, burnout, and compromised immunity, conditions that have become the norm in the developed world in the past few decades.

In his book *Why Zebras Don't Get Ulcers*, Stanford neurobiologist Robert Sapolsky, PhD, writes about the difference between the human stress response and that of animals: "If you are a normal mammal," he says, "stress is the 3 minutes of screaming terror on the savanna, after which either it's over with or you're over with."

I saw this play out on a daily basis by observing my dog, Champ. He wasn't on the savanna fighting off predators, just roaming his domain in my home and yard. Whenever the FedEx truck pulled up, Champ went berserk. His instinctive reaction began with a few growls. As the driver stepped out of his truck, Champ's stress levels went up. He started barking and scratching the door or the backyard fence. Champ had a singular focus: to defend his territory against anyone attempting to infringe on his domain. Once the package had been dropped on the porch, his "protect and defend" button switched off. Champ quieted down and all was well again. Dogs may be housebroken and domesticated, but they still have their protective instincts. By the time the truck pulled away from the curb, Champ was once again a playful pet gnawing on a chew toy, rolling in the grass, lying in the sun, or taking a nap, as if nothing had happened. He returned to his baseline, relaxed state very quickly. He expended no additional energy resenting the FedEx driver for stepping over the line or fretting that he might cross the line again.

ARE WE ALL WALKING TIME BOMBS?

After a tragic school massacre, the news quoted a classmate of the shooter describing the gunman: "He was fairly quiet and pretty much stuck to himself." Another student who'd hid in a classroom during one of these shootings told reporters the gunman was "a nice guy. I never suspected he could kill anyone." We hear family members or neighbors on the evening news say, "Yes, there were problems at home, but not enough to push him to do something like this."

Of course a man who shoots randomly into a crowd of innocent bystanders is driven by complex psychological components we can only guess at but never fully understand. I have witnessed many gentle, kind people who were not prone to violence suddenly blow a gasket one day and do something drastic. It makes me wonder: Are we all walking time bombs?

"We were never meant to deal with prolonged chronic stress," says Pamela Peeke, MD, of the University of Maryland. "The human body isn't designed to drag around bad memories, anxieties, and frustrations." But that's exactly what our bodies are forced to do. We're under tremendous pressure at work, at home, or sometimes both. Tension increases as unexpressed feelings build. Some of us have the skill to release the tension in adaptive ways: getting a massage, talking to a therapist or dear friend, spending an afternoon in nature or throwing ourselves into vigorous exercise. People who haven't found an outlet simply hold the tension in until their system breaks down and they can't take any more. They have entered a danger zone. People come home and let it out on their spouse and kids. Or flip out while driving, adding to the incidents of road rage.

Alan Keen, PhD, a behavioral scientist at Australia's Central Queensland University, asks the question, "Why are people in large cities more angry?" He goes on to explain, "If I'm living in a big city with a busy job and I'm multitasking and I'm a busy parent, all that translates into chemical changes in the brain." Chemical changes contribute to built-up anger, which comes out randomly in a public place as the individual dumps his or her rage at a stranger on an airplane or the waitress in a restaurant.

"Not me!" most people say. I used to believe that folks knew themselves well enough to recognize when they'd crossed the line into the danger zone, knew when they were at risk of rash action. This changed when I worked with a monk who'd spent 10 years living in a monastery. He reentered society, got into a violent argument with a woman, and was hauled off to jail. All those years of meditation had not allowed him to work through and release deep-seated rage toward a mother who had abused him as a child. He lived a peaceful life in the protected environment of the monastery, but once he was living among the public at large, his rage triggered, leaped out of his body, and jumped on a woman he'd started dating. Something she said or did, a moment of disapproval or anger, had flipped the switch on dormant feelings and they came alive. He lost control.

When we fill up with more emotion than the body is able to process and withstand, we need coping skills. Without a safe way to digest and clear bad feelings from the body, we are at risk of hurting someone or turning the rage in on ourselves.

I speak from personal experience. If I allow tension to build up or forget to breathe, move, or exercise, I can become run down. I might say or do something that I'll be sorry for afterward. I've said hurtful things. I have felt my jaw clench like a vice. I have even punched walls.

Fortunately I know how to defuse and de-escalate or remove myself from a situation now so I can keep it together and avoid doing something drastic. Here's an example.

I was heading to my hometown to give a talk at my alma mater, the University of Maryland. When the plane landed at Baltimore Washington International, I felt a surge of excitement in my chest.

As I watched passengers in the rows ahead of me begin to deplane, I grabbed my carry-on and waited my turn. The row in front of mine was clear except for one man who remained in his seat. I made eye contact and nodded "Go ahead," but he didn't move, so I stepped out of my seat and walked toward the front of the plane.

"Hey, man! How about letting people in front of you leave first," he said in a loud voice. He shoved me forward with enough force that I nearly stumbled into another passenger. Man, was I triggered. It was as if I'd been transported back to junior high school and an older boy—the bullying type—had just pushed me in the cafeteria line.

We can never know when old memories will activate and come to the surface. Everything we've experienced is stored in the intricate folds and electrical impulses in our gray matter. Certain significant events are tagged in long-term memory and become part of our life story, even our identity. As such, they typically retain a strong emotional charge. I must admit, I have a trip wire when it comes to bullies. For several moments thoughts of pushing him back and landing a solid one on the left side of his head raced through my mind. It was as if standing up to this man would cut all the bullies from my past down to size.

Seething anger pulsed through me as I rode down the escalator to baggage claim. I imagined pushing the man onto the carousel and shouting, "Take that, you bully. You have no right to push me." I caught myself and thought, "This line of thinking is not doing me any good. Stop stressing out. My family is waiting for me downstairs. Let it go."

I knew deep down that I would never accost the man. I just needed to shift gears. I sat on a seat at the bottom of the escalator and took a few deep breaths and practiced my rebooting technique, which you will learn in the next chapter. When I came back to my center, it occurred to me that the man must have been suffering emotional or physical pain to explode so quickly. I felt resolved, got up, and walked toward the carousel. I saw the man standing and waiting for his bags. I walked up to him and said, "I'm sorry about what happened back there. I thought you were waiting for someone or staying on the plane."

He replied, "F— you, man; whatever," and took a step toward me. His body was tense, as if he were carrying volumes of frustration and pent-up rage. I felt a cold, familiar fear. It was as if I'd never left junior high where guys like him would start a fight over just about anything. His face was red, his eyes angry and steel blue. I was flooded with familiar feelings and memories of getting pushed around by bullies.

I backed up and walked away, although I have to admit I

had a fantasy moment. I wished I was a black belt martial artist, so I could avenge every kid who ever got picked on or pushed around by a bully. My mind reeled through at least 10 heroic, cinematic episodes in about 2 minutes. I laughed to myself as I greeted my family.

This incident showed me, in a highly personal way, that the body-mind has a powerful stress response that can activate old memories. As a result, familiar feelings from the past resurface from similar events in real time.

When you are Whole Body Intelligent, you have a choice *and* the necessary tools to intervene when strong feelings flare up. You recognize that they have more to do with past hurts than what is happening in the moment. Whole Body Intelligence helps you make the best decision and take the right action. This is what happened when I sat down, breathed deeply, and allowed my body to talk to me. This incident helped me understand people who explode under duress only to be sorry, even shocked, at their behavior later.

PAPER TIGERS

Our instinctive, primal response to stress has not evolved as fast as modern-day society. Science verifies this: Studies demonstrate that our stress response fires an average of 60 times per day without much chance for recovery in between. The American Psychological Association conducted a national survey that found that one-third of Americans are living with extreme stress, and 48 percent of those surveyed report increased stress levels in the past 5 years. What's more, 80 percent of doctor visits are due to stress-related causes. This is, in part, due to an inability to shut off the stress response because we ruminate on events and worry that a similar danger might recur.

Lissa Rankin, MD, explains this from a physiological perspective in her book, *The Fear Cure*:

> All primal emotions, such as fear, hate, love, anger, and courage, arise from the amygdala in the limbic brain— the primal, animal part of the brain. This fear hub works in conjunction with the thalamus, which receives information; the cerebral cortex, which reasons; and the hippocampus, which remembers.
>
> Repetitive triggering of the stress response makes the amygdala even more reactive to apparent threats. Fear flips on the stress response, which triggers the amygdala—on and on and on. As this happens, the amygdala, which helps form the "implicit memories"— fragments of past experiences that lie beneath our conscious recognition—becomes increasingly sensitized and tinges those implicit memories with the heightened residue of fear. As a result, fearful feelings, often manifesting as feelings of anxiety, exist even in the absence of any objectively fearful experience.

The Chinese call this phenomenon a *paper tiger*: any event that appears in our inner world as terrifying but in reality is nothing to fear. In other words, we perceive a tiger, but the beast is a mere picture made of paper. The threat is illusory, generated by the mind. A paper tiger may appear to be perilous, but it can't eat you. If you believe it is real, however, your body will respond with a biochemical cascade of hormones that signal danger.

Dr. Rankin explains further:

> Simultaneously, the hippocampus, which is critical for developing "explicit memories"—clear, conscious recollections of what actually happened—gets worn down by the body's repetitive stress response. Stress hormones like cortisol weaken neuronal synapses in the brain and inhibit formations of new ones. When the hippocampus is weakened in this way, it's much harder to produce neurons, thereby making new memories. As a result, the chronic, painful, fearful experiences that sensitize the amygdala records get programmed into implicit memory, while the weakened hippocampus fails to record new explicit memories.
>
> When this happens, over time, you may end up feeling chronically fearful and anxious, with no real memory of why you are even afraid. You may feel an overwhelming pervasive sense of gloom and doom, as if something bad—something very bad—is threatening you, even though, to an objective observer, you appear safe. Even though long after the threat is over, anything that triggers this fearful response, consciously or unconsciously, stimulates the amygdala and retrieves the fearful memory from the hippocampus and suddenly, BAM. The body goes into hyper-drive. The trigger may not be directly related to the initial experience.

HITTING OUR LIMIT

"If I don't take a break from it all, I might blow a gasket," a 36-year-old client told me. I invited her to follow her inner compass, take a week off alone, shut down her smart devices, and relax, breathe, and walk a lot. She agreed she needed time to unplug and sort out the stressful issues in her life. She decided to go on a solo retreat and get some much-needed rest, perhaps at a place that offered massage services. It was time to reboot and chill. She left my office resolved: Yes, she was going on retreat to a spa on a beautiful beach somewhere. Two weeks later I got a phone call. Despite her clear intention, she hadn't taken that retreat but had increased her workload, which led to a flare-up with her boss that added more stress. She had finally been forced to rest when she had a heart attack and landed in the hospital.

This story brings home the following realities:

• The human body is not designed to deal with the type of prolonged, chronic stress so common in the technology age.

• The American Medical Association has identified stress as the number one cause of all human illness and disease.

• A large percentage of the population does not engage in proactive, healthy, body-centered methods to counteract the elevated stress levels we experience daily.

• Most people think of stress as something that comes from the outside. They focus on external problems and fail to address the roots of stress within their own body.

• A lack of effective stress management can cause a buildup of tension and unexpressed emotion, which can turn many people into walking time bombs that will eventually explode or implode in the form of disease.

Hans Selye, MD, studied the impact of threatening external events on an organism. Dr. Selye is known as "the Father of

Stress" because he coined the term and was the first to scientifically verify the existence of this biological response. He posited the first theories on stress while working on what was known in the early 20th century as general adaptation syndrome. His research showed that we have a limited supply of adaptive energy to deal with stress, and that supply declines with continuous exposure to stress.

WHICH VOICE IS LOUDER?

Our physiology sparks emotions. Those emotions influence our thinking. Those thoughts then act like gasoline we pour on our emotions, which continue to build combustion until they blow up in our body, affecting our physiology. This keeps going in a vicious cycle: Our physiology affects our thinking and feeling, which further impacts our physiology, which then comes back around and reinforces wrong thinking, and so it goes on and on and on.

Here's the physiological cycle:

- We have strong feelings that contain information.

- That information is stored throughout the body, not just in our mind.

- Every thought and feeling creates a physiological effect that occurs at a cellular level.

- The memory of this information exerts a profound yet largely subliminal influence on our perceptions, behaviors, and experience.

- Our perceptions and misperceptions generate more strong feelings.

Your body speaks to you directly in the language of sensations. Primary feelings are a crucial part of this language. Unfortunately, primary feelings are often lost to a wash of secondary emotion that is triggered by unresolved events or feelings from the past. It can be one word someone says, or a certain type of body movement they make, that takes us back to a painful memory or experience from the past. When we don't have a method for dealing with these emotions, they can lead to an anxiety attack, immobilize us, or throw us into uncontrollable rage.

JUGGLING TOO MUCH COMPOUNDS STRESS

The pressure we put on ourselves to get more done in a day than we possibly can, coupled with our reliance on smart tools, forces the brain to constantly switch between tasks. This overloads our capacity to process information. The result is burnout.

Professor Earl Miller, PhD, a neuroscientist at the Massachusetts Institute of Technology, scanned the brains of volunteers while they performed different tasks. What he found is quite interesting. When people are presented with a number of visual stimulants, only one or two of them tend to activate the brain. This suggests that we really only focus on one or two items in our visual field at time.

When we perform similar tasks at the same time (writing

someone an e-mail while talking on the phone with someone else), the two tasks compete to use the same part of the brain. Studies show that this common practice short-circuits the brain and sabotages us so we work less efficiently and eventually burn out. Some scientists go so far as to postulate that we can't and don't actually multitask, we merely jump back and forth between different neural circuits so fast that we barely notice that we stopped paying attention to task A when we switched to task B. If task A goes on automatic, even for a mere millisecond, we run the risk of making a mistake that cannot be undone, like pressing send on that e-mail we wish we had never sent. Additionally some studies show that many people have a stress response when they are unable to access their devices. Every experience "etches" neural pathways in our brain and central nervous system and stores corresponding information, sensations, and emotions in our body.

Even just thinking about multitasking can cause a change in your body. Glenn Wilson, PhD, a psychiatrist at the University of London, reported on this phenomenon a few years ago. Dr. Wilson found that being in a situation where you are able to text and e-mail at the same time—perhaps sitting at your desk—can knock 10 points off your IQ. This is similar to the head fog caused by losing a night's sleep.

This is why Dr. Miller warns against multitasking: "People can't do it very well, and when they say they can, they're deluding themselves. The brain is very good at deluding itself."

An American study reported in the *Journal of Experimental Psychology* found that it took students far longer to solve complicated math problems when they had to switch to other tasks.

In fact, they were as much as 40 percent slower when they switched from one task to another. The same study found that multitasking has a negative physical effect, prompting the release of stress hormones and adrenaline.

So not only does multitasking affect our mental clarity, but switching between tasks also makes us less efficient. This can trigger a vicious cycle: We work hard at multitasking, take longer to get things done, then feel stressed and harried, which compels us to attempt more multitasking. Once again we only have so much capacity before we break down and implode or explode.

Studies by Gloria Mark, PhD, an interruption scientist at the University of California, show that when people are frequently diverted from one task to another, they work faster but produce less. After 20 minutes of interrupted performance, people report significantly higher stress levels, frustration, workload, effort, and pressure.

The bottom line is this: Our high-tech addictions place an additional load of stress on our bodies. Being Whole Body Intelligent means you detect stress as it is building, before it wreaks havoc, and then choose to limit stressors like overusing smart tools and multitasking.

SEPARATION ANXIETY, CYBER-STYLE

I worked with an executive who had horrific anxiety attacks while taking a shower in the morning. His fear of missing an important transaction or e-mail caused tremendous stress whenever he didn't have his cell phone in his hand. Sound familiar? How many times have you turned around and driven the distance back to your home because you left your cell phone behind? How did you feel without it?

Tech Norms for Travelers, a survey conducted by Intel, found that 44 percent of American travelers become anxious without their computing device. Intel Newsroom calls our attachment to our devices "a deepening love affair" complete with an emotional bond that has a calming effect.

Is Intel Newsroom romanticizing our relationship with technology? You decide, in light of these survey results:

- Survey respondents ranked losing mobile computing devices when traveling as more stressful than losing their wedding ring (77 percent versus 55 percent).

- Travelers' cohabitation with their devices has become so pervasive that they admit they will go to great lengths to keep connected. Almost half of all travelers (46 percent) and 63 percent of young travelers admit compromising their personal comfort and hygiene in pursuit of a power source to keep their device charged. This includes going out of their way to find an available power outlet, choosing a restaurant or coffeehouse based on outlet availability, searching public bathrooms, or sitting on the floor near an outlet. Sixty-four percent of survey respondents admitted to sacrificing their personal appearance—giving up hair dryers or styling tools, toiletries, sunscreen, workout clothes, and even shoes—in favor of making space in their luggage for their beloved device.

Sure, we find ourselves more capable and connected by technology than ever before. As a result, when separated from our mobile devices, many of us experience the type of anxiety we would feel when separated from a loved one. This begs the question, Are we anxious about being separated from the iPhone itself or the people it allows us to stay in constant contact with?

My questions for you are, How addicted have you become to your devices? Do you spend more and more time in the cyberworld? How much heart-to-heart and eye-to-eye connection have you sacrificed in favor of chip-to-chip, silicon communication? Do you notice that your stress levels have gone up as you spend more time on the technology that populates your home?

Does technology consume so much of your time that you spend less time on physical activities that support your well-being?

Do you notice family members showing signs of social anxiety or impaired ability to communicate with others?

KIDS IN THE RED ZONE

Children's digital media expert Patricia Greenfield, PhD, told the *New York Times,* "You should wait as long as possible to get your kid a cell phone to maintain parent-child communication." I agree. Young kids raised with cell phones who play highly addictive electronic games as their main entertainment miss out on family fun time, shortchange their physical bodies and their social skills, as well as take on cumulative stress.

I had read in the *New York Times* and *Washington Post* and was told this when I visited Japan: A million Japanese, most of them teenage boys, live the life of a shut-in, avoiding all social contact except in cyberspace. They refuse to work and stay cloistered in their rooms for long periods—from 6 months to more than 10 years. Forty-one percent of these recluses lived in near complete solitude for 1 to 5 years. A government survey found that they spend most of their time in cyberspace because the real world is too stressful. How many socially inhibited and overstressed teens in the Western world never want to leave their rooms and may not? I wonder.

A study by the Kaiser Family Foundation revealed that the average kid listens to 2½ hours of music on their smart units each day, watches nearly 5 hours of TV and movies, spends 3 hours on Internet and video games, and accomplishes only 38 minutes of reading. That adds up to 75 hours of media every week. And that doesn't include the 1½ hours kids spend text messaging each day and the ½ hour they talk on the cell phone. The mobile phone is the device that makes this possible. Vicky Rideout, formerly with the Kaiser Family Foundation, says: "You don't have to sit down in front of a TV anymore and watch television at the time a show is broadcast. Kids can watch it on their laptop, in their bedroom. They can watch it on their cell phone on the bus to school."

In comparison, Blue Zone kids spend their days moving, actively engaged in a full range of community activities.

Cyberspace is largely a cognitive arena. Teens who spend most of their free time on one device or another will find it difficult to get out of their heads and into their bodies. This, in turn, inhibits their ability to feel and interpret emotions in a way that truly enriches their relationships with friends, family, and the world at large.

Think about it: A text message carries none of the nuance and emotional content that we experience when we hear someone's voice on the phone. Those of us who grew up with landlines remember what it's like to talk on the phone without a bad connection ("Can you repeat that? I couldn't hear you . . .") or the interruption of a dropped call. Even in good coverage areas, a mobile phone cannot deliver the fullness and subconscious satisfaction of linking with another via landline. I often find myself asking people if they have a landline so I can call them back from mine. It's amazing how my body relaxes when we make that solid, grounded connection. Try it and you'll see what I mean. Most young people have never had that experience.

Likewise, a photograph shared on Instagram, while provoking some feeling response in the viewer, does not allow for the fullness of sharing, comparing, and clarifying the meaning of the photo in the presence of one another. Before social media and Web sites replaced photo albums, we sat together on the couch to look at pictures, laughing, telling stories, and making the photo come alive by filling in the personal meaning and context represented in the picture. The development of relational intelligence—a foundation stone of our animal nature—is thwarted. The subtle signals communicated in body language, facial expressions, and those split-second micro-movements in the face that tell us so much about one another are lost in cyberspace. Even technological advances such as

Skype fail to satisfy our physical nature, which begs for human touch—a handshake, a hug, a pat on the back. Evolution did not prepare us for this type of systematic alienation any more than it prepared us to live underwater.

In little more than a decade, we have become high-tech beings, but evolution doesn't happen that quickly. Adaptation, yes. Evolution, no. Therefore, most of us get thrown off balance, physiologically compromised by a virtual mind-first lifestyle that leaves the body behind. The more cell phones, electronic tablets, virtual games, and computers dominate our lives, the more we build stress in our bodies. Physical activity and the refreshing exposure to nature falls by the wayside. We move less and stare at screens more. All the while, stress continues to build as the life of the body ticks away.

POOR POSTURE CONTRIBUTES TO STRESS, AND STRESS CONTRIBUTES TO POOR POSTURE

The technological revolution has also taken a toll on our posture. The human head weighs approximately 12 pounds when balanced above the spine. As the neck bends forward and down, the weight increases, placing greater demand on the cervical spine. At a 15-degree angle, your cervical spine must support approximately 27 pounds. At 30 degrees, 40 pounds. At 45 degrees, 49 pounds. At 60 degrees, 60 pounds. Our trapezius muscles kick in to compensate, which affects the back muscles. Overworked back muscles weaken the stomach muscles, which truncates the breath. Experts say it can reduce lung capacity by as much as 30 percent. This domino effect spreads through every part of the body.

"That's the burden that comes with staring at a smartphone the way millions do for hours every day," says Kenneth K. Hansraj, MD, chief of spine surgery at the New York Spine Surgery and Rehabilitation Clinic. Over time, experts say, this type of poor posture, sometimes called "text neck," can lead to early wear and tear on the spine, degeneration, and even surgery, all leading to more stress on the body-mind. "It is an epidemic or, at least, it's very common," Dr. Hansraj told the *Washington Post* in their November 20, 2014, issue. "Just look around you, everyone has their heads down."

Tom DiAngelis, president of the American Physical Therapy Association's Private Practice Section, told CNN last year the effect is similar to bending a finger all the way back and holding it there for about an hour. "As you stretch the tissue for a long period of time, it gets sore, it gets inflamed," he said. It can also cause muscle strain, pinched nerves, or herniated disks. This unnatural compression degrades the neck's natural curve.

Poor posture can cause other problems as well.

Posture is affected by the failure to exercise—to move and bend, to push and lift, using our musculature as we have over millions of years. Core strength suffers, making it harder to hold our head high. The human body is designed to stand strong and erect, effortlessly. Poor posture leads to back pain and digestive problems. Our hips and knees don't get the interplay with gravity needed to make enough synovial fluid to keep our joints lubricated. Lymph flow is slowed. Oxygen-poor blood doesn't get pumped back to the lungs with efficiency. Sleep suffers, memory has more lapses, and our vital energy gets depleted. Poor posture has been linked to headaches, neurological problems, depression, and heart disease. This cascade of ill effects contributes to social issues such as absenteeism and the rising cost of health care.

Our bodies and minds can only recharge when we flip out of stress mode and correct some of the habits covered in this chapter.

When you are Whole Body Intelligent, you are more aware of the stress response, which means you can catch it and address it sooner. This enables you to take charge and intervene by shifting out of the stress mode at will. WBI also alerts you to stop dwelling on scary scenarios and come into the present moment, to the life of the body.

In the next chapter, you will learn how to accomplish this by employing a key component of WBI, the rebooting technique. You will learn and practice seven effective steps to redirect your stress response and calm rather than aggravate your nervous system. This is how you master stress instead of letting it master you.

CHAPTER 6

THE REBOOTING TECHNIQUE

HIGH-SPEED INTERNET, CLOUD COMPUTING, online shopping, 24/7 connectivity on multiple platforms—how does human evolution keep up with these unprecedented advances? How can you protect your body so you won't get overwhelmed, cyberaddicted, or completely burned out?

In my private practice and trainings, I've been helping people understand and manage their stress for decades. I've also worked closely with medical practitioners and their patients. For the past 4 years, I've worked at the Preventive Medical Center of Marin, north of San Francisco, as part of their integrated approach to wellness. A core part of what I add to the physicians' programs is teaching patients my seven-step stress-management protocol that I call *the rebooting technique* (TRT). We have seen amazing results in the way people's health improved and how it helped the doctors understand more about their patients (i.e., breath patterns, destructive beliefs, trauma held in the body, and so on). One of the physicians calls TRT his secret weapon because of the information he gets from me. So I wanted to put TRT to the test and get empirical evidence of its effectiveness. I am glad I did.

Three medical doctors—Elson Haas, author of *The Detox Diet*; Richard Shames, author of *Thyroid Power: Ten Steps to Total Health*; and Michael Rosenbaum, president of the Ortho-molecular Health Medical Society—contributed to the study, which was conducted by Ernest T. Hubbard, a cell biologist, biochemist, and genetic scientist specializing in stress and vitality. Hubbard employed leading-edge diagnostic tools that measure stress and heart rhythms for the study.

I knew TRT was effective. I've seen the positive impact it's had on me, and on many people who use it, many times. What I did not know was the profound and measurable effect TRT can have on human physiology.

Hubbard began the study conducted at the Preventive Medical Center of Marin in San Rafael, California, by comparing patients' heart rate rhythms before and after doing TRT. Consistently, I watched as the lines of the diagnostic machines jumped all over the place, up and down—the very picture of a nervous, anxious person. After 5 minutes of doing TRT, the line undulated up and down evenly.

Then, we measured changes in the patients' stress levels. The chart (opposite) shows the coherence ratio of a patient in the study. *Noncoherence* is a typical pattern of someone undergoing high levels of chronic stress—when the mind and body continue to operate in "fight or flight" mode even if there is no overt stressor present. The coherence ratio here would show strongly in the low range. Conversely, the healthy and natural rise and fall of our heart rate is called *coherence*. When someone achieves coherence, they generally enjoy a reduced overall heart rate; reduced fatigue, anxiety, and stress; and enhanced digestion, sleep, and mental awareness. A coherence ratio in optimal conditions is 100 percent high. Therefore, when the coherence ratio goes up in the high range, this is a good sign.

TRT has been shown to enable an individual to rapidly move from a continuous noncoherent mode to a normal coherent mode. This makes it possible for the person to function neurologically, physiologically, and physically as a normal healthy human being. Overall, patients who employed the rebooting technique while hooked up to diagnostic machines for just 5 to 7 minutes reduced stress on an average of 55 percent and changed erratic heartbeats to coherent ones.

THE REBOOTING TECHNIQUE (TRT) RESULTED IN A 55% REDUCTION IN STRESS

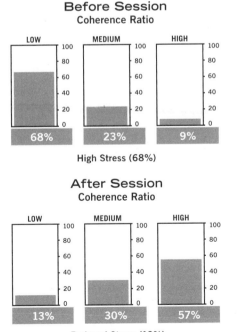

Study conducted at Preventive Medical Center of Marin, San Rafael, CA

CYBER PAPER TIGERS

We are not getting our ulcers being chased by saber-tooth tigers, we're inventing our social stressors—and if some baboons are good at dealing with this, we should be able to as well. Insofar as we're smart enough to have invented this stuff and stupid enough to fall for it, we have the potential to be wise enough to keep the stuff in perspective.

—ROBERT SAPOLSKY, PHD

Some evolutionary psychologists believe that evolution doesn't necessarily require extended periods of time to leap ahead but can occur between generations. This is evidenced by the ease with which youngsters navigate an iPhone, iPad, Droid, or Kindle Fire. Beginning in kindergarten, or even earlier at home, children have access to computers. High school kids get their homework, report cards, and test results online. They can look up a class syllabus or review the week's assignments on their smartphones. I recently heard a story about a 3-year-old boy—illiterate, no less—who picked up an iPad and immediately started to swipe between apps as though he were playing with a pile of Legos.

But what of the baby boomers—the Steve Jobs and Bill Gates generation—who were "smart enough to have invented this stuff" in the first place? How do they wise up to the social stressors their generation invented? And what of Generation Y, born between 1981 and 1994? Some of them fell so far into the cyberworld that they became Internet addicted before they reached the legal age to drink. How do they unplug and "keep the stuff in perspective"?

People born after the late 1990s—the Millennials and now Generation Alpha—never knew a world without the Internet. And yet their physical bodies did not evolve to live in a world dominated by silicon-based communication. When my parents came home from a hard day's work, they spent time with the family. No smartphones. No e-mails. No notifications or Tweets or Snapchats. Their lifestyle gave their minds and bodies a chance to rest and recharge before the next work day began.

As inventors, consumers, and purveyors of technology, we have to get better at dealing with the stress. We need to find and implement the best practices to keep our minds and bodies in top form given our accelerated lifestyle. Your single most valuable asset in this regard is your attention.

ATTENTION IS LIKE THE SUN

Attention may be one of the most overlooked engines of success. Attention drives everything you experience. The way you move about the world and navigate your relationships depends entirely on where you place your attention. All of your experience is influenced, nourished, and regulated by your attention—whether you realize it or not. Consider an important relationship, perhaps an old friendship or a business associate that you have nurtured and cultivated over the years. Attention is what grows our relationships and delivers the value of connection. The same is true of your relationship with your body.

Think of attention as your internal sun. What you direct your attention toward is what gets illuminated. Attention is fickle, however—it is not necessarily selective about where it goes any more than sunlight is selective about where it lands. But, like sunlight, attention can be directed and harnessed to our advantage.

TWO KINDS OF ATTENTION: OUTWARD AND INWARD

Your attention has two primary pathways or directions in which it can travel: inward or outward. Most of us tend to prioritize external stimuli and allow what's going on "out there" (exteroceptive) to dominate our attention. We pay attention to our colleagues and supervisors at work, our to-do lists and grocery lists, our children and spouse, our bicycle or basketball or personal trainer. These external pleasures and pressures demand our attention and captivate our senses. Most of us pay far less attention to the world that lies within, the world that establishes the tone—happy, sad, tranquil, irritable—of our day-to-day lives. We are compelled to turn our attention inward (interoceptive) when we experience strong feelings, pleasurable sensations, physical or emotional pain. Your attention goes outward when you sit down to a wonderful meal. It goes inward when you savor the flavors or push the plate away and say, "I'm full."

Withdrawing our five senses from the external world and turning them inward has profound physiological effects on the body. In Eastern philosophical and spiritual traditions, this turning inward is the key to inner peace and the kind of happiness that prevails regardless of outer circumstance.

Researchers discovered that the brain's frontal lobe is not the sole source of attention as was previously believed. People were asked to engage interoceptive attention by focusing on their breath, or to use exteroceptive attention and focus on words placed before them on a screen. What the researchers found is intriguing. Exteroception primarily involves the frontal lobe of the neocortex (evolution's most recent innovation), whereas interoception reaches deeper into the brain to the older, limbic system by activating what is called the limbic bridge. In lay terms, this means that when we focus on the outer world, our perceptions are conceptual; i.e., framed by specific abstractions or beliefs. On the other hand, when we focus inwardly, we rely on parts of the brain related to sensation and integration of physical experience. These deeper parts of the brain are not governed by our self-concept and are free of social constructs such as "How do I measure up to others?"

Have you ever felt anxious and wished your mind had an off switch? No matter how hard you try to stop the racing thoughts, your mind won't let go of whatever it's riled up about. Experience tells you that "this too will pass," but your best efforts to relax and let things unfold just get you more knotted up. You can try to talk yourself out of being angry or anxious, but talk is not only cheap in such cases—talk is worthless. Problem is, the frontal cortex is an inept watchdog for an unruly mind.

That's the bad news.

The good news is, interoception and the neural networks and brain structures it involves may prove to be the built-in shutoff valve for the flood of racing thoughts. The frontal lobe is prone to overthinking things, but we can learn to ride those rapids and lean into our interoceptive awareness to find a place of calm.

REBOOTING

Tom was against a deadline on a monster project. He'd been up since before dawn searching the Internet, updating Excel sheets, compiling PowerPoint slides, editing video clips, and creating a playlist for his presentation. Needless to say, the desktop on his computer was overcrowded. He had 12 windows open in one browser, 5 in another, and was running 6 different programs at once.

He'd been ignoring his hunger pangs for 2 hours when he decided to step away from his desk and make some breakfast. When he hit "save" on the Excel sheet he was working on, his screen froze. The mouse was dead. His keyboard was useless. His monitor was blinking back and forth between pitch black and the "blue screen of death."

Tom chuckled, remembering the first time this had happened to him years earlier, before he'd become facile with computers. He'd nearly gone into a full-blown panic attack but gritted his teeth (Tom hated asking for help) and rung up his friend, Al, a supergeek. When Tom explained what he was seeing on the screen, Al muttered, "When was the last time you rebooted your computer?"

"How do I do that?" Tom had asked. He smiled to himself

at the memory. He could still hear Al's musical accent as he explained, "First turn off the computer, then the modem, then your router. Then unplug all power cords from the back."

Tom did exactly what Al had suggested. He watched his monitor go black, heard his computer wind down, and watched all of the lights on his modem and router fade away. He pulled the power cord out of each device and told Al, "Okay. It's done."

"Now flip the switch on your surge-protector strip. You want the red light to go off so you are powered down."

Al told Tom to make sure all the plugs going into the strip were firmly connected, to look for anything irregular about his hardware setup such as frayed wires. In other words, he told Tom to observe—to check out the surrounding area and note anything unusual.

"Nothing unusual," Tom reported.

"You're ready to reboot," Al said.

That was the first time Tom had heard the word, but he knew instantly what it meant. "Reboot? You mean turn it back on? That's all there is to it?"

"Sometimes," Al said, "if you have a lot of windows open or programs running, you may have run out of RAM. Or maybe the registries need to reset. It doesn't really matter exactly what was wrong. Nine times out of 10 the reboot will fix it."

"More like 99 times out of 100," Tom thought. Like most of us, he's been unplugging and plugging in his device countless times over the years. He doesn't even watch to make sure the system will reboot—he's come to trust the process implicitly.

Like Tom's computer, our bodies can get so congested and overwhelmed by inputs that our bioprocessor hits max capacity. We get fried and burn out. Our system crashes or freezes up. When this happens, we need to go through a step-by-step sequence such as Al offered to Tom to reboot ourselves.

When you boot up your computer, you load the operating system into working memory or RAM. When computer science was in its infancy, the equivalent process was called "bootstrapping," as in "pull up by the bootstraps." Once personal computers caught on, the term was shortened to "boot." To boot up or reboot a computer means to access the run time environment necessary for normative operations. We power on, the machine locates and initializes peripheral devices, finds and loads the operating system, and—ta da!—we're up and running.

There are times in our lives when we need to reboot—to shut down long enough to refresh and revive before we make our next move. The best practice is to schedule a reboot on a daily basis before we get stuck and frozen or follow the wrong path for too long. It's just like when you reboot a computer: You notice when basic operations start to slow down and get sluggish, and so you reboot to regain the desired processing speed. You're not making any changes to the hardware, just giving the software a chance to reestablish smooth operations. When you reboot yourself, you do the same.

But you don't have a power button or a Force Quit command for your body-mind. You can't simply hit

Control+Alt+Delete and shut down. There's more to it than that.

Rebooting yourself takes a commitment of time. As with a computer, you don't press the power button off, then instantly turn your machine back on. You have to pause, give the device a chance to get ready for what's next. That's what you need to do for your body-mind as well.

I have my clients set aside 5 to 7 minutes for the rebooting technique. Busy executives typically tell me they don't have 5 minutes to spare, and yet they will find that 5 minutes if their computer freezes!

Initially you may think it's a waste of time to slow down and reboot yourself. Once you get up and running again, you will see the reboot's positive effect on your mood and performance.

We all know the feeling of getting stuck—that unproductive zone that finds us slogging through and making little progress. And yet we force ourselves to keep going. Thinking becomes muddled, decisions are hard to come by, problem-solving skills go on strike. Then your mood may tank, your head starts to pound. Your ability to relate to coworkers, to communicate clearly—any number of ordinary operations begin to fail. Worse, if you don't know how to get unstuck, you waste more time.

Getting unstuck is a skill set. One you can build and strengthen over time. The next time you find yourself trudging through difficulties, give yourself a reboot. Take a page from technology and Force Quit whatever is going on so you can fire yourself up again.

KEEP UP WITH YOUR WORLD USING TRT

You're at work. You just got wind that your spouse's company is discussing a merger and your spouse could lose his or her job. You feel emotion building. You might hit a wall and thus stop working on the exciting proposal you and your team need to get out by the end of the day. Instead, since you are Whole Body Intelligent, you have the foresight to sidestep the impact and say to yourself, "Time for a reboot." By the time you go through the steps outlined below, you'll be in better shape physiologically, mentally, and emotionally. You'll feel centered, better able to focus. The potential layoff situation might still exist, but the stress load will be lifted off your body and you'll have the clarity you need to make your next move.

TRT is an intervention tool because the technique has you step in and interrupt your spinning thoughts and steer them away from rather than into an unproductive loop-the-loop. We all know the futility of spinning out in unproductive, repetitive thoughts, but how many of us have a reliable alternate route? That's what this technique gives you—a new approach that puts the body first so you can get relief and perspective for your mind.

The rebooting technique is a popular warmup for athletes before workouts or games, a way for entertainers and speakers to get relaxed and present before an important event, and a booster for anyone before engaging in a social event.

When I sit offstage before giving a talk and hear the host or emcee start to introduce me, I quickly go through the seven

TRT steps: step 1, step 2, step 3, and so on. By the time I walk onstage, I'm at my best.

Daily Peak Performance Practice

In addition to using TRT as a way to intervene in high-stress situations or warm up before an important event, I recommend using the technique daily as a meditation. Transcendental Meditation practitioners get tremendous benefit from two short 15-minute sessions of meditation each day. With WBI you use your breath and body awareness as the points of focus rather than a mantra (sacred sound).

I have worked with nonprofit organizations and corporate teams who made a commitment to using TRT daily. After doing TRT twice each workday, an executive team I worked with at eBay experienced lower levels of stress and reported feeling better equipped to solve problems. TRT, when practiced by a couple, partners, or a group, opens neural pathways for higher-level thinking and improved communication between people.

YOUR SYMPATHETIC AND PARASYMPATHETIC NERVOUS SYSTEMS

The rebooting technique both reduces stress and opens the door for creative thinking by relaxing the autonomic nervous system. When we are stressed, the sympathetic, fight-or-flight nervous system is dominant. Heart rate increases. The liver pumps out glucose instead of bile (because you'll need a boost of energy to run from the tiger). In fight-or-flight mode, your pupils dilate, as do the air sacs in your lungs, and your digestive system shuts down (this is not the time to eat). TRT allows the parasympathetic nervous system to reengage and balance, calm the body, and turn off the emergency brain-stem functions. This is, in large measure, what gives TRT its power.

Just as when you reboot a computer, with TRT you need to disconnect, to let your system shut down so that all the static charges roaming around can dissipate. As any techie will tell you, a computer reboot is all about the sequence and getting a clean signal. It's the same with the autonomic nervous system; we need to restart in the right way to effectively reengage with other people.

Sequence is everything. It's important to perform the TRT steps in order, to go back to the fundamental body-first approach that is your grounding cord. That solid foundation is essential. It gives you balance.

When you look at healthy mammals or well-trained athletes, they are neither totally stressed nor totally relaxed. They are somewhere in the middle. That is the ideal state for high performance. It can be called coherence, or balance; in the world of music, we call it harmonic.

After a successful reboot on the computer, you're ready to go. The wireless network is reconnected, the programs are humming along, RAM is available, and the bulk of your work is stored on the hard drive. You sit, fingers poised above the keyboard. Before you touch the mouse or strike the first key, the computer is in ready mode. It's not sleeping, it's not trying to process more than it can, its circuits are not burning up. It's waiting there in neutral, ready to process information you need.

TRT is a bit like human tech support. When you get stuck or find yourself running out of energy, when you simply cannot look at one more task on your to-do list, it's time for the rebooting technique. As a techie would say, your system is designed to work. There are no missing parts; what you have is a software problem, not a hardware problem. Reboot yourself to restore balance and alignment and to be poised to take on a rich, fulfilling life.

The Rebooting Technique Step-by-Step Sequence

1. Unplug	5. Adjust
2. Breathe	6. Visualize
3. Observe	7. Reboot
4. Report	

Let's dive right into the entire technique in sequence. I'll review the rationale for each step and guide you through the execution of that step. Before long you'll have the seven steps mastered—and then who knows what you can accomplish.

Step 1. Unplug

The word *plug* originated in the 17th century from the Dutch word *plugge* for a stopper used to seal a barrel or other container. When a container was plugged, the fluid was retained.

The risk of loss from spillage, evaporation, or overflow was eliminated. To "unplug," then, means allowing the contents—be it wine or water or grain—to pour out of the container and be utilized.

In the context of electronic devices such as computers, to unplug means to remove the device from its source of power. While unplugged, the device is completely disconnected from the source of electricity. Until reconnected, it cannot interface with the rest of the world. (For the purpose of this comparison, let's forget about batteries.)

In the context of humans, the act of unplugging is similar in that it involves doing our best to shut down and disconnect from powerful distractions and stressors of the moment. Said another way, we step back and get some distance so the stress doesn't push so much voltage through our body and mind. To do this, we eliminate, as much as possible, all outer stimuli—noise, bright lights, even tight clothing, and certainly interaction with others. We unplug to achieve a state of insulation from the outside world. This need not take a long time: A brief interlude can have a beneficial effect on your heart rate, as we have seen. This simple act makes space for expanded awareness and enables the reflective ability of the individual.

Setting aside the time needed to unplug is an essential first step in the process. We need time to disengage from the stressors, distractions, and demands of life in the moment so we can delve into the inner layers of awareness that restore balance.

When we unplug, the adrenal glands produce lower concentrations of the stress hormones cortisol and adrenaline. When stress hormones in the blood drop to normal levels, the nervous system turns the corner and starts to make its way back to a calm state—to rest and digest rather than fight or flee.

Try this now: Take a few minutes and disconnect from the outside world and all of its pressures as completely as possible. Commit yourself fully to the process. Shut off the phone, close the door, do whatever you need to free yourself up so you can direct your attention inward for 5 minutes. Eliminate or minimize all distractions and begin to redirect your attention inwardly to your emotional world and your physical body.

Step 2. Breathe

Countless scientific studies have demonstrated the link between stress and breathing. Common patterns such as shallow breathing and shortness of breath show up consistently when someone is under significant stress. Sustained periods of short breathing, coupled with rapid heart rate, can result in increased blood pressure, accumulation of toxins, and hormonal imbalances.

In short, conscious breathing is essential for harm reduction given the many stressors we confront in our lives. We breathe consciously by bringing our awareness to the physiology and feeling of our breath. We pay attention to the otherwise unconscious activity of drawing air into our lungs and releasing it. We can use our imagination to augment and hone our senses by allowing our mind's eye to see the heart and lungs working in unison to drive vital oxygen through the bloodstream and carry waste products out in the form of carbon dioxide.

People who are chronically stressed are typically not aware of their respiration at all. In the extreme—a panic attack, for example—a person can actually lose the ability to breathe.

Try this now: Take three slow, deep, full breaths in through your nose and exhale each time through your mouth. Relax. Fill your belly on each inhalation. Release the breath and belly as you exhale. Feel free to sigh or yawn or make a sound as you exhale. Loosen your jaw. Let go of all expression on your face. Relax.

Step 3. Observe

The word *observe* is derived from the Latin *observare,* "to watch." To observe is to notice, to perceive, and to register some phenomenon with our primary five senses. We have this marvelous ability to discern, detect, and spot both the subtle and the not-so subtle details of what is going on around and within us.

A key to observation that allows for keen discernment is sensing what is, as it is, without an added layer of preconception or judgment. For example, you might observe a political or religious rally and fixate on your judgments—positive or negative—of the people involved. If you were to completely detach and suspend all judgment, observing the same event might lead to very different conclusions. Tests conducted of eyewitness accounts have proven that our ability to observe is strongly influenced by our preconceptions as well as the stress load we carry during observation.

You can see, then, the importance of taking time to unplug and breathe to enable you to clearly observe your mind, emotions, and body. Observing your body from a relaxed state of elevated awareness can reveal layers of your physical and emotional state that otherwise go undetected. You might, for example, note that your posture is asymmetrical or your legs are tightly crossed.

Try this now: Scan your body from head to toe. Notice what is happening. Are you squinting or straining in any way? Are your shoulders and neck crunched? Observe for at least 60 seconds and discover sensations, check your posture, and notice any tension you feel, etc.

Step 4. Report

The word *report* is derived from the Latin *reportare,* meaning "to bring back" and "be accountable."

In step 4 you are encouraged to report and declare your observations aloud or to yourself, to bring your awareness into play and be accountable. Putting words to your observations gives credence, confidence, momentum, and accountability to the process.

Try this now: Report what you notice in your body—either speak it out loud so you can hear your own voice, or say it silently to yourself. Tell yourself what you notice. For instance, "I am noticing that my breath is shallow and my fists are closed." Or "I am noticing how relaxed my belly and chest feel."

Step 5. Adjust

Step 5 is literally to take action. For example: If you observe and declare that your fists are clenched, you adjust by consciously relaxing your hands. Or if you observe and report that your legs are crossed while you are standing and you realize that this puts you in a vulnerable position that broadcasts "I'm not 100 percent sure of what I'm saying," your adjustment would be to uncross your legs, place your feet squarely below you, and find symmetry in your posture or stance.

By acting, adjusting, and moving during step 5, you complete the circle from the initial unplugging event to "plugging back in"—this action clears the static in your body-mind and allows it to reconfigure and effectively reboot your entire system.

Try this now: Now that you have unplugged, connected with your breathing, observed your body, and declared your observations, it is time to take action and adjust your body. For instance, if you notice that your shoulders are raised, relax them and let them drop. If you are hunched over your computer, sit back and lift your head. Take 60 seconds or longer and do whatever your body needs.

Step 6. Visualize

Derived from the Latin *videre,* "to see," the word *visualize* means to form a mental picture of something. Step 6 is the mental counterpart for the physical correction you accomplished in step 5. Now you allow your imagination to see a perfectly rebooted you.

The chemicals produced in the mind with this type of visualization can be extremely therapeutic and empowering. By doing this consistently over time, you can reduce inflammation in the body and boost your immune system.

Try this now: Take a minute or two and visualize yourself, your mind, and your body in this very different state from when you began TRT. Notice if you feel more connected to yourself. Imagine a wave or wave form, and slowly breathe in and out.

Step 7. Reboot

The seventh and final step is to "bring it all home," recognizing that in these past few short minutes, you have:

- Unplugged from life's stresses

- Settled your system down in preparation for inner observations

- Observed and declared aspects of your body, mind, emotions, and world

- Made constructive adjustments in what you observed

- Visualized yourself in a new and improved state for reentry into the world

Try this now: Take a moment and decide on the next purposeful action you want to take. (Even taking a hot bath when you are stressed is a purposeful action.) Identify your top priority in the moment, stay focused on your intention, and go do it!

Rebooting your "system," much like rebooting your computer, should be done with care and consciousness, as you watch your ducks line up in a row.

The seven simple steps of TRT become more and more natural for you as you do them. You'll become better at this body-mind troubleshooting with practice.

Move fluidly through the steps, summarized in the box on the opposite page.

When you have finished all seven steps, pause here a moment to notice any feelings or sensations. From a body-first approach, what is your experience of the world around you as you take it in now?

If you would like to practice TRT with me and/or print out a PDF of the steps, visit this online link for readers: WholeBodyIntelligenceBook.com/TRT.

If you wish to read the entire report of the TRT study, go to WholeBodyIntelligenceBook.com/TRTstudy.

Now that you are equipped with TRT, you are ready to step into the next leg of your journey: using your ever-increasing self-awareness to tackle the number one modern-day culprit and silent killer: chronic stress.

THE REBOOTING TECHNIQUE

Step 1. Unplug

Find a few minutes and disconnect from the outside world and all of its pressures. Locate a quiet, comfortable place where you will not be interrupted.

Step 2. Breathe

Concentrate on your breathing, inhaling slowly through your nose and exhaling through your mouth. Do this three times. On each exhale, loosen your jaw and let your mouth drop open.

Step 3. Observe

Scan your body from head to toe. Spend at least 30 seconds or more to inventory your body experience—body sensations, tensions, posture, etc.

Step 4. Report

Report what you have noticed in your body—either speak it out loud so you hear your own voice, or say it silently to yourself.

Step 5. Adjust

Allow your body to return to a natural, relaxed state by moving in some way that shakes off or reduces tension. If, for instance, your shoulders are high up near your ears, relax and lower them.

Step 6. Visualize

Now for a minute or two, notice if you feel more connected to yourself. Imagine an ocean wave or a wave form in your mind's eye as you breathe slowly in and out.

Step 7. Reboot

Decide on the next purposeful action to take. Identify your top priority in the moment. Inhale and exhale with one more conscious breath, stay focused on your intention, and go do it!

PART III

TRANSFORM LIMITING BELIEFS

CHAPTER 7

THE ISSUES ARE IN YOUR TISSUES

No matter how successful you get, it's really difficult to shake your mind-set. And I still have a poor person mentality. I can't shake it. And it gets really detrimental when you can't just shake off the idea. When I go to sleep at night right now, I am as financially nervous as I was 20 years ago.

—WILL SMITH

ACTOR, PRODUCER, AND RAPPER Will Smith made the above statement to Oprah in 2010 after she asked him why he gave his oldest son, Trey, the book *Rich Dad, Poor Dad* to read. Will Smith's net worth was $240 million that year—not the kind of income that would cause someone to have a "poor person mentality."

Smith, aka "the Fresh Prince," had earned his first million by the age of 19. He parlayed his success as a recording artist into the title role of a hit TV series. Once he had the attention of Hollywood, Smith's career shot into the stratosphere. He holds a number of box office records, has been nominated for four Golden Globe Awards and two Oscars, and has won four Grammys.

His family is like entertainment royalty. His wife, Jada Pinkett Smith, has been in the entertainment industry for 2 decades, starring in movies such as *The Matrix*. Their two children, Jaden and Willow, are enjoying skyrocketing careers. Jaden appeared in *The Pursuit of Happyness* with his dad and had the starring role in *The Karate Kid* remake produced by his parents. The film earned $360 million at the box office. Daughter Willow's hit song, "Whip My Hair," rose to number 11 on the Billboard Hot 100 and garnered her a BET Awards nomination for video of the year.

Objectively speaking, Smith and his family have enough money to last lifetimes. But his subjective experience doesn't match up. He still worries about finances every night when his head hits the pillow.

Of course, Oprah and her audience were surprised by Smith's courageous revelation. I imagine that many viewers assumed he'd grown up poor and could appreciate his fear that he might end up back there someday. That's what I wondered too: "Perhaps his parents struggled to make ends meet and he still carries fear from how it was back in the day?"

I was wrong. Smith was raised in Wynnefield, a middle-class neighborhood in west Philadelphia. He told *Essence* magazine that his dad "was an independent businessman. He set up refrigeration in supermarkets, and he always provided for us. He's a steady and positive figure in my life." Smith's mother worked for the school board of Philadelphia. Smith attended the best school in the neighborhood, Our Lady of Lourdes, a private Catholic school. He graduated from Overbrook High with high enough grades to be admitted to the Massachusetts Institute of Technology.

So how does a man who had these advantages and subsequently rose to fame at a young age get "a poor person mentality" that he can't shake? My coaching experience told me that something shook up his nervous system around money. I thought to myself, "I've seen this with clients. They know conceptually and factually that they have plenty of money, but the stress response that got turned on in their body at some point gets retriggered again and again whenever they think about finances."

Smith's confession piqued my interest. I surfed around on the Web to see what else I could learn about his past, especially concerning finances. Here's what I found.

The Fresh Prince had released three popular rap albums by 1990. He found himself an instant millionaire and quickly stepped into a jet-set lifestyle. He bought a mansion near Philadelphia and a fleet of expensive cars. His closets were full of designer clothes, and he often treated his entourage to expensive dinner parties and extravagant trips.

On *Inside the Actors Studio* in 2002, Smith talked about his reckless spending habits and his problems with the Internal Revenue Service. He appeared on *60 Minutes* in December 2007 and revealed to Steve Kroft that the IRS eventually assessed a $2.8 million tax debt, took many of his possessions, and garnished his income. Smith went from being a millionaire to nearly bankrupt in the course of a single year. To make matters worse, the entourage who'd tagged along for the ride all but disappeared. When he ran out of money, his friends ran out on him.

Will's megatalent, drive, and ambition enabled him to generate tremendous wealth and more than make up for his financial losses. And yet, by his own admission, the fear of financial problems still lingers. From a Whole Body Intelligence (WBI) perspective, the trauma of an experience like Smith's gets etched into the cells of the body. The experience and the memory of going broke live on in his body and, like so many of us, he just couldn't shake it off. No matter how much money he made, he still went to bed nervous.

FACT VERSUS FICTION

Will Smith knows he is rich, and yet his body still has him on edge at times. The fact is, he has plenty of money, but his body doesn't always know that. Like Smith, many of us carry beliefs that mess with our lives and jangle our nerves. As he clearly stated, "it gets very detrimental when you can't just shake off the idea."

You bet it does. I've seen what he described play out numerous times. I've met fit and trim folks who tell me they still feel self-conscious about their weight when they go out in public. This "idea" they can't shake off has a negative effect both socially and in business. I've met with gorgeous, vibrant people who tell me that they feel like an ugly duckling when they walk into a party. They leave events early or avoid people because social contact causes tremendous anxiety. I've had brilliant software inventors with genius IQs confess that they always feel like they are the dimwit in the room. I've helped charismatic inspirational speakers who struggle with self-doubt when onstage or become hypercritical when they see themselves in a photo or video. They go through hours of anxiety before they hit the stage. And I've coached extremely talented athletes who practice with confidence but freeze up when they are close to winning. They lose the last set in tennis or choke in the closing minutes of a basketball game.

Conditions such of these are often rooted in past experiences. A chubby kid got ridiculed in grammar school. A 13-year-old girl who broke out with bad acne was told by her older brother that she was ugly. A star pupil failed a test or didn't get into an Ivy League college and his father told him he was stupid. A young man found that women were less attracted to him once his hairline began to creep toward the crown of his head. A football star lost his girlfriend the day after winning the state championship. Experiences such as these don't just live in our memory bank, they literally live in the tissues of the body.

I know how confident I am when speaking to an audience and yet, out of nowhere, my body might send me a memo to "watch out" in the form of butterflies in my belly. On the one hand, in present time my mind is excited and confident, but my body is following another, older story line. It remembers when my cousins and I left our inner-city neighborhood for the first time and were harassed and chased home by a bunch of bullies from the other side of town. Even though speaking to a group is safe and not at all like being chased home, it still rings a bell and brings up the old belief that "it's not safe outside my comfort zone." Fortunately today I know this belief is not true. I also recognize how it feels in my body, so I can head it off at the pass—before it builds up momentum—and ultimately walk onstage completely relaxed.

HOW BELIEFS EMBED IN OUR BODIES

When we get hurt and are unable to resolve and process our emotions through the body, the emotions and hurts linger. They don't magically disappear. We kept them at bay by holding our breath and squeezing them into our bodies, but they never expressed all the way through. It's like putting a load of wash in the machine but never letting it cycle through to rinse and dry. The clothes get funky. For instance, when my cousins and I got home from that terrifying expedition beyond the neighborhood, I was afraid to tell my parents what had happened. So I forced a tight, strained smile and held back the tears. Had I gone ahead and told my mom and dad about the episode, let the tears flow, felt their empathy and concern, and received their comfort and protection, my intense feelings would have completed their life cycle and been resolved in the presence of understanding and love. Since I held in the feelings and did not express and release them, that emotional energy had to find a place to hide in my body. My brain stem and nervous system absorbed the impact in the form of a limiting belief that got seeded in my body: "New places out there are not safe."

What can you do to prevent bad experiences from embedding in your body-mind as limiting beliefs? And how can you deal with the ones already in place? In Chapter 6 you learned how to use the rebooting technique (TRT) to intervene in stressful moments to center and calm yourself. You also learned how to destress *before* an important event using TRT to relax your nervous system.

Your next step to becoming Whole Body Intelligent is to uncover and examine your sabotaging beliefs—those ornery culprits that live in your body and unpredictably surface and attack you. If a limiting belief is particularly strong, it delivers a dangerous, powerful punch that may lead to destructive behavior and poor choices.

If you had a tumor, a parasite, a virus, or an infection in your body, you would do whatever it took to eradicate it. I view destructive beliefs the same way. The sooner you can detect, examine, understand, and disarm them, the better!

So let's talk more about beliefs. To keep things simple, we'll categorize them as either *viral* or *vital*.

Viral Beliefs

I coined the term *viral beliefs* to reflect the toxic effects of negative beliefs. Like infective, corrupting agents that sicken our bodies, viral beliefs sicken the mind and negatively impact behavior. Just like those pesky, parasitic, protein-coated virus molecules, viral beliefs can lie dormant until some external factor or emotional trigger activates them.

Most viral beliefs are falsehoods, distortions whose power lives in the past. Unfortunately that power exerts itself in the here and now when dormant emotional energy activates and reenacts the emotional trauma that was implanted in the body when the original insult occurred. Viral beliefs are not true in the present moment, but they sure do feel real. Because you believe a viral belief is real in that moment, your body responds with the same biochemical signal it did in the past, saying that you are in danger and that you need to protect yourself as best you can. Unfortunately the strategies we employed to protect ourselves in the past can redouble the difficulty in the now. As long as viral beliefs go unexamined and live on in the body, they can trick you into acting in counterproductive ways.

Since we often don't detect viral beliefs when they are operating, they can cause conflict, mistrust, and other problems in our relationships. They can assert themselves in our body language and send messages we are not aware we are broadcasting, messages that are contrary to our true intent.

That's usually the case when we feel perplexed because we lost a sale we thought was in the bag, or when we get rejected for a second date that we thought for certain would happen. That's how devious viral beliefs are: They can disrupt our personal and business relationships without our knowing why. They show up in our body like a big billboard that transmits incongruent and misleading messages to others. We say one thing with our mouths while our bodies say something altogether different with posture and movement. We appear to the other person as inauthentic.

Vital Beliefs

The dictionary defines *vital* as lively, energetic, animated, and needed by your body in order to keep living. A vital belief benefits your body and mind, supports your goals, and enriches your relationships. Vital beliefs play opposite viral beliefs. Say "No!" to viral beliefs and "Yes!" to their antidote: vital beliefs.

It's a simple formula. Having more vital beliefs and fewer viral beliefs makes for a happier, less stressed, more empowered, and healthier you.

THE WAR DRUMS OF VIRAL BELIEFS

I participated in my first Native American sweat lodge many years ago on New Year's Day. The sweat was led by Charles Thom Sr., also known as Red Hawk, a medicine man of the Karuk tribe from Mount Shasta. We met at Samuel P. Taylor State Park, about 40 minutes north of San Francisco. When the sweat participants arrived, we were led to a clearing alongside a creek where a dome made of willow branches had been constructed. Covered with blankets and tarps, the small dome resembled a mud hut or igloo. I entered and sat on the cold mud floor. I shivered in the dampness. When Red Hawk gave the order and his assistant brought hot rocks into the hut, I welcomed the warmth. Then Red Hawk threw water on the rocks and signaled for the blanket door flap to be closed. Suddenly the lodge was dark and steamy. The smell of winter was strong all around. I felt pleased to bring in the New Year singing Native American chants in a sacred lodge.

Red Hawk asked for more hot rocks. We sang and we sweated. More hot rocks, more water, more steam, more singing, more sweating. After 45 minutes I began to feel restless. The heat was getting to me. My mind was racing: "It's too hot, the hair on my arms is burning, I hope the heat doesn't scorch my lungs, my heart is really pumping. When is he going to open the damn door?"

I remained silent, but Red Hawk sensed the group's restlessness as the sweat lodge got hotter and hotter. He stopped chanting and said, "Your medicine man feels your uneasiness. You have a war dance going in on your minds. Get down low to the ground and touch the earth and let your mind go." I followed his instructions. I got out of my head and into my body.

The coolness of the earth against my body calmed my mind within minutes. The ceremony was easy from that point on. I left the lodge an hour later cleansed and inspired from the many visions I experienced during the sweat.

Red Hawk knew that the way to instantly stop the war dance of fearful and unhealthy thinking in the mind was by forcing a shift in focus. Engaging my body and feeling the cool ground made a biochemical alteration in my brain that quieted the war drums of fearful thoughts beating inside.

It's the same with viral beliefs. They are constantly running your life and creating a war dance in your body-mind, interfering with your ability to create positive desires that you have for yourself. With your whole body's intelligence, you can take charge of your mind and dig deep inside your body—in your cells, in your tissues, wherever you stored these viral beliefs. Once you identify where they live, you can bring them to the surface and diminish them. That makes room in your body to receive and "embody" new, vital beliefs in their place. I have seen lives change for the better from doing this.

EMOTIONS AND CELLULAR MEMORY

In her popular book *Molecules of Emotion,* neuroscientist Candace Pert, PhD, formerly of the National Institutes of Health, explained:

> Emotions are cellular signals that are involved in the process of translating information into physical reality, literally transforming mind into matter. Emotions are at the nexus between matter and mind, going back and forth between the two and influencing both.

Dr. Pert's research confirms that emotions are stored in the cells of the body as a cellular memory. And this is what she says about bringing about changes at the cellular level:

> My research has shown me that when emotions are expressed—which is to say that the biochemicals that are the substrate of an emotion are flowing freely—all systems are united and made whole. When emotions are suppressed, denied, not allowed to be whatever they may be, our network pathways get blocked, stopping the flow of the vital feel-good unifying chemicals that run both our biology and our behavior.

That's exactly the problem we address in this section. That's why WBI shows you how to express blocked, denied emotions; free up the biochemical substrate that is stuck in old patterns; and release the flow of feel-good chemicals and hormones such as serotonin.

Consider this story. Anita came to the Preventive Medical

Center of Marin, California, for a second opinion on persistent stomach pain. Her primary physician had ruled out an ulcer and told her to consult with a surgeon about laparoscopic surgery to remove her gallbladder. She came to PMCM to explore alternative approaches before resorting to surgery. She met with a doctor who reviewed her medical records and had a long talk with her about lifestyle, exercise, and eating habits. He completed a medical examination and recommended a custom program consisting of a special diet and supplements. He also recommended she see me as part of her treatment. He believed that the way she managed stress was affecting her health and exacerbating the stomach pain.

We all develop specific ways to manage stress (a glass of wine after work, a vigorous run, hobbies, sports, all sorts of soft and hard addictions) to give our mind a break. At work we might use complaining as a pressure-relief valve. In relationships we might argue to blow off steam. Some of us internalize stress; this is called somaticizing—turning anxiety into physical symptoms that affect various parts of the body.

When Anita walked into my office, I immediately noticed a troubled look on her face. She began to tell me how worried she was all the time. "Why do I get this pain in my belly? It's driving me crazy, not knowing the cause. Why me?" She paused. I nodded to assure her I was listening and encouraged her to continue.

"What if surgery doesn't fix the problem?" she said. Her body was also talking. She crunched down, put a hand on her belly, and asked, "Who will take care of my daughter if I'm not here?"

These were valid questions for someone considering surgery, but I sensed she was carrying other big hurts and fears in her belly—emotions that had been brewing for some time. I acknowledged everything she said and explained that I didn't have specific answers but maybe her body did. She was game.

I began by asking her to take a couple of breaths in and out. Anita took a few rapid short breaths from high in her chest. I showed her how to breathe deeper and slower and suggested she observe her breathing for a few moments. She nodded her head in agreement. She then tried to take a few deep breaths as I'd instructed. Anita found it difficult to breathe in deeply, but she found it even more difficult to let go on the exhale.

Generally, when people have difficulty letting go on the out breath, it correlates with a lack of confidence, especially when they tend to avoid saying things that are difficult to say. This holding in is mirrored in the breathing pattern. When I commented on her labored breathing, Anita reported that it had become increasingly difficult to breathe for the past several years, even before she started having pain in her stomach.

I prompted her to allow her belly to expand as she inhaled. She closed her eyes and put her hands on her stomach as I'd demonstrated. Less than 2 seconds later, she opened her eyes and flared, "It's too hard. I don't trust my body. In fact I don't trust much nowadays. I just want to quit." I waited a few moments. She continued by insisting, "Saying what I feel won't get me anywhere. I'll end up sick and alone anyway."

That was a defining moment. Anita had spoken aloud a deeply held belief. I repeated what she'd said back to her. She looked at me and sighed. Her breath flowed out easily. I took this as a good sign that she was ready to go to the next step and suggested we look together at how that belief might be affecting her health and other aspects of her life.

I asked her to repeat "Saying what I feel won't get me anywhere; I'll end up sick and alone anyway" several times while pressing on the area of her abdomen where she felt pain. After speaking this a few times, tears started rolling down her face. She switched to saying, "You hurt me. You hurt me," several times in a row as a memory she had tried—unsuccessfully—to forget for many years came to mind.

Ten years prior she'd been a rising executive who'd just been promoted to VP of human resources. Her employer was a giant in her industry; her career dream had come true. Her father, a college basketball coach, had instilled in her a deep sense of team spirit and loyalty. She was devoted to her job, working day and night. She always felt run-down and missed time at home with her daughter. But she was her father's daughter, so she put her head down and worked herself silly in order to save enough money to pay her daughter's college tuition.

One afternoon the board dismissed the president of the company and brought in a new CEO. She knew the new president. She had worked with him when he was an independent consultant for the company. It was her job to meet with him and renew his employment contract. When she did, he made an unusual request. He asked her to maintain his current status as an independent contractor and continue to pay him as per his existing contract for another year. She was surprised by this request, especially coming from a man who would be heading up the company. Anita explained the legal ramifications: To do so would leave the company vulnerable and jeopardize her standing as an HR professional. She explained, "With all due respect, sir, I could get penalized by the IRS and the company could get in trouble for illegal employment practices."

Anita was fired for underperformance a few weeks later. She sued for unfair termination but was shocked when coworkers she considered friends appeared in court and lied about her job performance. Even her best friend, who was her daughter's godmother, testified against her. A number of grueling, extremely stressful months in court followed. Bit by bit she lost all faith in people. Her lawyer had forbidden her to discuss the case with anyone. She remembers the strain of holding her shock and rage in her belly as her former friends, one after another, took the witness stand and told blatant lies. She was overwhelmed by the stress of court proceedings coupled with an inability to say anything to her friends. She told me, "I don't think I've been able to relax my belly since that happened 10 years ago."

Our work together allowed her to recognize a strong negative belief that she'd been holding in the recesses of her belly since the day the trial began. She described the feeling as "a big block of sludge that's been sitting there for years." I prompted her to touch, breathe, and listen to her body and put words to this block of sludge. She took her time, moved her attention into her belly, and then uttered these words: "Trusting my gut will get me into trouble, make me sick, and push away my friends." I told her, "I can see why you'd think that, especially after being fired for doing the right thing." I also shared that she was at a choice point. "This is an opportunity," I told her. "You can hang on to those thoughts, stay stuck in the past, and continue to stuff your feelings about how much that hurt. Or you can express your feelings and notice what happens in your belly."

Anita chose the latter option. As she breathed in and out, touching the sore spots in her belly, I invited her to give voice to whatever she was holding in her gut. She started off slowly: "I could have gotten in trouble by keeping my mouth shut." I encouraged her to speak a little louder and say everything she hadn't said to the new president and her former friends and colleagues at the company.

I suggested she take herself back to the courtroom and speak to each person, one by one, telling them what she felt and how much their betrayal had hurt. As she did, her belly pain started to decrease. She continued to breathe and feel her emotions. After a few moments, she stood up and shouted, "How could you lie about me in court?" Her voice grew louder and louder until she screamed, "And you! You were my daughter's godmother. Where were you when I needed my best friend?" Her body started shaking. I asked her to continue. "All you cared about was your fancy home and your off-the-charts clothes budget. Do you have any idea how much you hurt me?" Then she started blasting the company top brass. "I worked 16 hours a day and ran your HR department by the letter of the law, and you fired me for it." I acknowledged her courage to express her truth. I witnessed her standing tall and telling each person how she felt. By the time she was done, she was taking full, deep breaths. She looked lighter; the haggard look on her face was gone.

In subsequent sessions she continued to voice years of unexpressed feelings she'd kept buried down deep. Within months she reported to her doctor that her daily stress and her belly pain were gone for the first time in years.

Her kind heart beamed through her eyes. Her veil of stress, caused by holding old hurtful feelings in her body, was gone. She looked more relaxed in general. She said she felt like herself once more.

Within months she began to trust again. She felt ready to get back to the work she loved. She now holds an executive position with one of the largest Web-based businesses in the world. And she can work from home frequently to be close to her daughter.

By expressing her viral belief and "shaking out" the repressed emotions associated with that belief, Anita got her energy, and a whole lot more, back.

"GOT TO CLEAR BEFORE WE CAN CURE"

Meet Kay Corpus, MD, a bright young doctor who owns and directs the Center for Integrative Medicine in Henderson, Kentucky. Her approach to medicine involves finding the root cause of illness and symptoms, which she believes is essential to health and healing. She states, "In my practice, we not only work on discovering why physical imbalance occurs, but why emotional, psychological, and spiritual imbalances occur as well." Her philosophy stems from this guiding principle by Caroline Myss, the thought leader and author who believes our biology is a result of our biography.

Dr. Corpus, a board-certified family physician, a fellow with Andrew Weil's Arizona Center for Integrative Medicine, and the former director of integrative medicine at Owensboro Health Regional Hospital in Owensboro, Kentucky, is also a certified Whole Body Intelligence coach. Dr. Corpus has used the WBI process to release limiting beliefs with several dozen patients, and she sheds light on the process that Anita and others go through when they discover and release viral beliefs: "We use WBI techniques for identifying and dispersing beliefs with our patients because we learned we have to clear the limiting beliefs and blockages in the body before we can really cure."

I met Kay Corpus at Lissa Rankin, MD's physician training, for which I am a faculty member. Dr. Corpus wrote a blog after taking the WBI class I gave at the training. That blog enlightened me even more about the power of beliefs to affect our health, well-being, and more. Here is what she wrote:

> In Steve's session he asked us to close our eyes and tune in to our breath, attentive to rhythm and quality. He asked if it was harder to breathe in or breathe out. Never noticing before, I felt a glitch on the inhalation. He then asked us to scan our bodies, identify

the most intense sensation, and then infuse deep breaths at that particular spot. Immediately, I felt a piercing pain between my shoulder blades! He asked me ever so calmly, "What is underneath the pain? What emotions or thoughts lie beneath it? What are your shoulders saying to you?" Out of nowhere authority figures appeared in my mind pushing me to be more, do more, faster and better. Then a loud and vivid voice that seemed to come from my shoulders said, "I have so much to do and I can't do it all by myself!"

Though a little freaked out by what came up, I knew that was true. Doesn't the saying go, "We carry the weight of the world on our shoulders"? Well, my shoulders were tired and they hurt! And maybe the reason I had trouble inhaling was because I couldn't (or didn't want to) receive help. "I have to do it all by myself" was my limiting belief. Yet I couldn't carry the burden of having to do *everything,* without my body, my shoulders, feeling the consequence. This is how the body gives (not-so) obvious clues! The pain lessened just as I made the realization *to ask for and receive help.*

Inspired by my own experience, I began using this technique on my patients. The results were amazing! One patient freely moved her neck after 3 weeks of stiff, painful torticollis (twisted neck). She realized that the unexpressed anger and disappointment at her daughter who chose inheritance money over their relationship froze her ability to "turn the other cheek" so to speak. As she expressed her emotion, and her viral belief, she released her pain and immobility.

Another patient, positive she had a ruptured disk, demanded an MRI for thoracic back pain that had gotten worse over the last month or two. There was no recent injury or trauma. She already had consulted the orthopedic surgeon, physical therapist, osteopath, and chiropractor with no diagnosis or relief. I asked her to examine deeper, *underneath* the back pain. Tearfully, she admitted constant rescuing of her adult child from bad choices stressed her out and kept her emotionally and financially (as well as physically, I may add) restricted from doing things she wanted to do. She realized now that she needed to let her daughter live her own life, including making her own mistakes. Remarkably, her back pain disappeared . . . right then. She walked out of the office with ease, deferred the MRI, and planned to schedule a well-deserved vacation.

The more I used WBI techniques in my work, I began to realize how essential it is for us, as health-care providers, to embrace and utilize less physically invasive methods and more emotionally excavating techniques with patients. Uncovering and mobilizing the trapped stories, emotions, and limiting beliefs patients hold in their bodies gets to the *root* cause of the problem. What may present itself as a migraine, pelvic pain, or recurrent sore throat in the doctor's office is often not, or at all, the end of the story.

Dr. Corpus holds the vision that medical professionals everywhere will add this type of deep inquiry to patient clinical assessments. She states, "Think how more efficient diagnosis, treatment, and healing could be? There is surely a time and place for conventional modalities, but the majority of cases could benefit from this unique body-centric approach."

Beliefs in the Body

After reading her blog, I wanted to know more about Dr. Corpus's insights on the WBI belief process. In an interview, she explained what had occurred for her. When she'd tuned in to the tightness in her shoulders, she actually saw an image and had a visual memory of her parents that revealed a deep-seated fear. In her words, "It was astounding. Intellectually, I knew that my emotions could get trapped in my tissues, but I had never experienced it directly. By embracing and focusing on a certain body part, I actually saw an image and felt what I was carrying in my shoulders. Images came up of my parents as authoritative figures, repeating over and over, 'You should be doing this.' I got very clear in that moment that I didn't want to carry those past memories around. Feeling the physical sensation of pain and what was underneath that pain, then breathing, acknowledging, and releasing the pain, was the missing link. It's the extra piece to healing I was looking for in medicine."

Dr. Corpus brought up another important point. Medical doctors have only a limited amount of time and resources. Most are trained to give a medicine or a pill. Many don't have time to include emotions and explore the psychological root cause of a disease.

Similar to Dr. Pert's perspective, Dr. Corpus believes that unprocessed emotion can contribute to the disease process by feeding pathology. She thinks the future of medicine "will use body-centric processes to infuse new life into the areas in our bodies that need to move the stuff out that's just packed in there for years."

WHAT ARE SOME OF YOUR VIRAL BELIEFS?

In the next chapter, you will come face-to-face with your erroneous limiting beliefs that may stand in the way of fulfilling your potential and acting in your own best interest. Viral beliefs often attach to our deepest desires. Beneath your genuine desire to reach a particular goal, you may have a subconscious self-imposed limitation that tricks you into thinking and acting against your own grain. The WBI belief process can help you unearth the beliefs that distort your perception and influence your actions, like it did for Anita and Dr. Corpus.

Before we jump into the next leg of this adventure, take a moment and reflect on any obvious self-sabotaging beliefs that you want to face head-on.

Take a few deep breaths originating from your lower belly in through your nose and out through your mouth and answer these questions.

What is one positive change you would like to see happen in your life? _____

_____

What do you feel in your body when you visualize actually having what you want in your life? _____

_____

Are you aware of a voice in your head or a body sensation that holds you back and stops you from believing you can have what you want? _____

_____

Does it stop you from taking effective goal-oriented action?

_____

_____

Finally, how committed are you to finding and clearing any viral beliefs that stand in the way of your dreams, goals, and happiness?

25% _____

50% _____

100% _____

OTHER% _____

Let's turn the page now and dig deep inside and change some limiting beliefs.

CHAPTER 8

IDENTIFYING AND CHANGING VIRAL BELIEFS INTO VITAL ONES

I was exhilarated by the new realization that
I could change the character of my life by changing
my beliefs. I was instantly energized because I
realized that there was a science-based path that
would take me from my job as a perennial "victim"
to my new position as "co-creator" of my destiny.

—BRUCE LIPTON, PHD, *THE BIOLOGY OF BELIEF*

LIKE BOB DYLAN SANG years ago, the times they are a-changing. Science, technology, and ancient wisdom were once far apart, but in recent years the gap between these disciplines has become smaller and smaller. New data from scientists such as Bruce Lipton, PhD, has afforded us a fresh understanding and appreciation for the wisdom of the ancients and of so-called primitive indigenous cultures.

Until the 1960s the Western world dismissed or outright

rejected philosophical systems and spiritual practices that did not share the predominant worldview. Then the Age of Reason shook things up. We began to question science and the fixed position of "If you can't prove it, it doesn't exist." As Eastern philosophy, with its emphasis on the body and transcendent knowledge, infiltrated the West, we started asking more and more pointed questions. And modern-day scientists met that challenge by pulling up their bootstraps and embracing the unknown.

Neuroscientist Jane Foster, PhD, of McMaster University leads a team that has been studying depression. Dr. Foster says, "It might be time to start thinking about treating depression from the bottom up instead of the top down. We have empirical evidence that the brain is responding to the gut. Let's make that the therapeutic pathway."

A *New York Times* article titled "Themes of the Times: General Psychology" reported the following: "Research has found that the gut has a mind of its own [called] the enteric nervous system. Just like the larger brain in the head, researchers say this system sends and receives impulses, records experiences and responds to emotions." The article quoted Michael Gershon, MD, professor of anatomy and cell biology at Columbia-Presbyterian Medical Center in New York, as saying, "Research shows that the enteric nervous system mirrors the central nervous system."

There's a renaissance happening—a shift from a more rigid, "solid" way of thinking to a more liquid, flowing approach that is open to new ideas and possibilities. Scientists, techies, and thought leaders are working toward a common goal: boosting consciousness so we can keep up with the technological explosion that defines our time.

We are seeing a new synergy between science and the non-ordinary realms—the transcendent, the transpersonal, and the mystical, i.e., flashes of genius (think Einstein), creative genius (think Steve Jobs), and miraculous healings (think cancer remission brought about through prayer). The emerging *integral paradigm* offers powerful insights and tools to help us understand ourselves.

Moreover, we are being liberated from outdated beliefs held by the collective that affect each of us on a very personal level.

As an example, take the work of Dr. Lipton, a former medical school professor and research scientist. Dr. Lipton was fascinated with the mechanisms by which cells receive and process information. In his book *The Biology of Belief,* he challenges one of the collective beliefs we have heard our entire life: We are controlled by DNA. Dr. Lipton asserts that the notion that we are less powerful than our genes is a fallacy.

He cloned cells and found that even cells that had the genes removed still had control over their behavior. That suggests that humans have a track to run on other than genetic determinism. What if our genes alone do not control our biology? What if we can change what we thought we had no choice about due to heredity?

This raises the question, does our DNA control us or do we control our DNA?

Consider the case of a man whose parents are both obese.

He is convinced that his fate is sealed, but Dr. Lipton's work and that of many others show that this man is not limited by heredity. Said another way, his choices and attitudes play a major role in genetic expression. Of course he will have to take 100 percent responsibility for his health, his dietary choices, and his activity level. But the bottom line is, he cannot convincingly shift the blame to his parents or his genes alone.

Dr. Lipton's research suggests that our DNA is strongly influenced by our environment and picks up signals from *outside* the cell. He posits that our thoughts are actual emanations that transmit positive or negative energetic messages that, in turn, affect genetic expression.

Of course, certain traits are genetically determined and immutable—eye color, hair color, skin color. But thoughts, attitudes, and beliefs are within the scope of personal choice if we are willing to take on that responsibility, be proactive, and rewire our brains and beliefs.

HAND-ME-DOWN BELIEFS

According to Dr. Lipton, for the first 6 years of life we are in a trancelike state. During this time our belief systems get downloaded from our environment. This environment of course includes the "big people" around us, who tend to hold a boatload of beliefs, many of which go completely unexamined.

The individual psyche absorbs these beliefs and takes them as a given; they are assumed to be matters of fact rather than matters of perspective. As children we are like sponges soaking up the worldview, beliefs, and assumptions of our family, community, and culture. But these attitudes, mind-sets, and beliefs are maladaptive in the larger world to the degree they contain misinformation, biases, and inaccurate points of view.

Hand-me-down beliefs can exert a strong influence on our lives. This isn't a problem if the influence is positive: say, for example, a belief that compassion toward others is essential to a life well lived. However, if the beliefs are negative, short-sighted, judgmental, or ignorant of the facts, they generate all kinds of chaos and untold suffering. If we are intent on rising above these negative beliefs, we need specific body-mind anti-virus software. And that is what this chapter has to offer.

VIRAL OUTBREAKS DUE TO TRAUMA

The human psyche is extremely impressionable. When we get hurt, a part of the brain never forgets it. Evolution built this feature into us. On a physical level, it's how we protect ourselves from further injury, even death. On a psychological level, it's how we avoid unpleasant consequences and threats to our physical and emotional well-being, our self-esteem, or our place in the community. Most of us experienced hurtful, even traumatic events in childhood: physical or emotional abuse, injuries, parents getting divorced, siblings dying, or moving away from childhood best friends.

Traumas become viral beliefs or feed existing ones. In cases where the trauma is repeated or ongoing, these beliefs can mutate and become particularly virulent.

All it takes is one moment, one sideways glance, one comment.

One summer night I was leading a sing-along around a campfire at a gathering in Oregon. I noticed a girl about 5 years old. She was mesmerized by my guitar playing. When I took a break, I called her over. I held the instrument toward her and asked if she would like to play it. Her chest opened wide and her body started shaking with excitement. I handed her the guitar, gestured for her to hold it on her lap, and showed her how to strum the strings. She took to it immediately and began to sing and make up a song. She threw her head back and started to rock out. Then it happened. In a flash her father swooped down and shouted, "Hey! Put that thing down and stop making so much noise!" Her mom joined in, "I wouldn't be singing with that voice, honey."

That's all it took.

The little girl's body language went from expansive and excited to crouched and wounded. In that moment she was inoculated against creative expression. An emotionally charged reprimand like that translates in a child's mind as, "When I sing and play music, I am only making noise and bothering people." Her parents had essentially injected this viral belief into her. I saw and felt the virus spread through her body as she slumped down and dropped her gaze toward the ground, unable to deflect her parents' disapproval. She looked up at me, and her eyes were so, so sad and full of shame. It was as though a beautiful songbird had hit a sliding glass door and was lying paralyzed on the ground.

A single event like that can stop us cold. Remember, at that early age, we are in a semitrance; we look to our parents, our authority figures, to give us the lowdown on who we are and what we can or cannot do in life. Their view of us informs our sense of self and where we belong. If they squash our creativity, our love of music or art, or any other fantasy endeavor, we may struggle to find our passion or vocation later in life.

The irony is, the belief that little girl took in not only hurt her, but it wasn't true.

Her parents returned to their adult conversations, oblivious to the effect they'd had on their daughter's body and mind. I crawled over to her and whispered, "You were great. You have real talent. When you get older, play and sing with all your heart." It was my way of attempting to depotentiate the virus.

I still think of that little girl on occasion and pray the vital belief I offered her was stronger than the viral belief that said, "Don't you *ever* sing and play guitar." After all, some birds fly smack into a glass window, hit the ground, then quickly recover from the shock and fly away.

Unfortunately, negative messages are thrown at young people all the time. They are like darts that strike a bull's-eye in the vulnerable human heart. Sadly, most of us don't have someone nearby to deflect the dart.

CLEARING VIRAL BELIEFS WITH WBI

Rita is an executive known in her business community as one of the best at what she does. She is an innovator in her industry, well respected and loved by those who work for her. Rita declared an intention for our work together: She wanted to know if something inside her was holding her back. For quite some time she'd been in line for a promotion to VP of a leading technology company. She richly deserved the promotion—her colleagues told her so at every turn—and yet the goal had eluded her.

To demonstrate the Whole Body Intelligence belief process, I'll walk you through what Rita did to turn her viral beliefs into vital ones.

Here is a quick overview of the four-phase process.

1. In phase 1 we employed the foundational components of WBI that you learned and practiced earlier in the book. This helped Rita shift her attention away from her external environment and the constant buzz of her busy-bee brain and onto her body by bringing her awareness home to scan, report, and adjust what was happening in her body.

2. In phase 2 she stated her desire aloud then observed and reported on her body's response. She gathered important information from the emotions and beliefs that arose when she stated her desire.

3. In phase 3 she identified and processed her viral belief. We worked together to disentangle it from her desire.

4. In phase 4 Rita began replacing her viral belief with a vital belief.

Rita arrived for her appointment with her iPhone held to her ear. She quickly wrapped up her business call and tucked the device into her purse. Her shoulders were slightly pulled in toward her chest as if she were protecting herself. She looked uncomfortable in her body—an especially telltale sign. I knew straightaway we had work to do so she could step into a powerful leadership position in her company.

I asked if she'd be willing to turn off her cell phone for the duration of our session, explaining the importance of taking a break from the outside world. She agreed.

I began by suggesting she shift her attention from everything that happened before she arrived and put her attention completely on what's happening in the present moment. I suggested she do this by observing what was going on in her body without judgment. This was the beginning of Rita's journey within.

"Take three deep, slow, belly breaths in through your nose," I continued. "With each exhale, let your mouth and jaw relax, and say 'Ahhhh.'"

This would help her bring her awareness inside, I explained, and thus connect her to her whole-body experience rather than to what she was thinking. I asked her to notice anything she could about her breathing pattern. Was it was easier to inhale or exhale? Where did the breath originate in her body? Did her shoulders move with the breath? Her rib cage?

After a few breaths, she reported that it was more difficult to breathe out; the exhale seemed to get caught at her breastbone. I asked how it felt to pay such close attention to her breathing. She replied, "It's a new experience, but I feel like I've actually landed in my body. It's been a long time."

I suggested she keep breathing consciously and informed her that often when someone discovers that their exhalation is more challenging than their inhalation, that correlates to "holding things in" versus expressing freely. She nodded several times in agreement. She was connecting with her bodily experience.

Next I asked her to scan her body from head to toe and report her observations out loud. I guided her, saying: "Rita, notice the sensations in any part of your body—tension or tightness; tingling, vibrating or twitching; pain or discomfort; a pleasant sense of relaxation; perhaps even hot or cold sensations. Then declare what you notice out loud. Describe each sensation. When you are ready, say, 'I notice _____.'"

After a few moments, she reported that her shoulders felt very tense, as if she were trying to make herself disappear into her chest.

"Are those feelings familiar to you, Rita?" I wondered aloud.

When she nodded yes, I asked her to place her fingertips where she felt the most tension in her shoulders and to do her best to breathe into that spot. "Have the breath come up and touch your fingertips," I instructed.

As she did this, her emotions started to rise and tears flowed down her cheeks.

I asked her what happened. She reported, "I saw myself as a young girl. I grew up with five older, bigger brothers in a traditional Irish family. Boys were always more important than girls." Her brothers were all much bigger, she explained. They bombarded her incessantly. They would tease and ridicule her, saying, "You're a girl. You're stupid. You're clumsy.

You can't play with us." If Rita cried, they called her a crybaby and told her to get lost. If she got angry, they laughed at her and said, "What are you going to do? Tell Mom? Tattletale!"

Rita described it this way: "It was the five of them against me all the time. I had to just take it because if I reacted, things got worse. I had no defense against them—and I was extremely vulnerable. Their attacks really got under my skin. I started to believe them, thought I wasn't smart, couldn't do sports, would never be as popular or confident as them. I also took on their point of view that all I was good for was helping my mother in the kitchen. They even hoodwinked me into doing their share of the chores.

"Whenever they were nice to me, even if it was only for a brief moment, I was so happy," she added. "I was convinced they were smarter than me so if they approved of me, I must be okay. But most of the time, I just went numb and did everything I could to be as invisible as possible so they would leave me alone."

Rita had carried a self-image of "I'm inferior" into her adult life. While in college, she wrote a paper about her brothers and how they'd treated her. When she let her parents read it, they became angry and upset. She kept quiet after that, until she came to see me decades later.

She'd never fully realized that her body had responded to these experiences by curling in to make her smaller so she would not be seen.

Rita clearly was making contact with her body, so I moved

to phase 2 and invited her to continue to breathe and feel as she focused on what she truly wants in her life.

I guided her, saying: "Visualize and feel your desire, the thing you want most in your life right now. Breathe in deeply through your nose and out through your mouth. As you inhale, imagine that you are breathing into your body the very thing you desire. Feel it saturate every cell, and anchor your desire in your body. Now state your desire with total conviction."

Rita took a few moments and said, "I want to be recognized for who I am. I want to be a vice president in my company." I asked what she felt in her body as she said this. She reported that she felt herself get small and collapse as she spoke the words.

I had her combine her desire and what she felt in one sentence. She said, "I want to be recognized for who I am as a vice president, and I feel tension in my shoulders and start to collapse and make myself disappear." I had her say this three times in a row. Her shoulders starting twitching, and I encouraged her to let them talk.

"Exaggerate any movement you feel, allow any instincts and urges to surface spontaneously and be expressed," I urged. "Make sounds if you wish. Express everything through words, sounds, and movements."

She started moving her shoulders and shouted, "You are wrong about me. I am not just a dumb girl. You have no right to criticize me."

After several minutes Rita said she felt more freedom and space in her shoulders, as if she'd shaken a bit of the grip her brothers had on her sense of her worth.

UNDISPUTED TRUTHS THAT TURN OUT TO BE LIES

Rita was ready to move into phase 3 and identify the viral belief that was stopping her from getting what she wants. She contemplated for a few moments and said, "I'm not smart enough to achieve what I deserve."

Rita's memory kicked up a collage of thoughts, images, feelings, and body sensations. She remembered her college days, when she felt tremendous fear that she wasn't as smart as other students, reasoned that she had to study twice as hard as her peers, and pushed herself beyond her physical limits during final exam week. She had a vivid memory of getting the flu one year after finals. She was able to connect the feelings and sensations with fears she felt now in her professional life, and the belief that she must work long hours to get the job done. "I'll never be good enough to be seen as a leader in my field," she shared. Rita had never put these beliefs into words and shared them aloud. I instructed her to repeat that limiting statement several times: "I will never be on top of my game because I'm not as smart as other people. There are always men who are way smarter than me, who know things that I don't know." Each time she vocalized it, she felt more relief.

Rita carried a belief that male VPs were innately smarter and more competent than her. She was quick to shift blame, albeit subtly. "After all, my brothers convinced me of that pretty well."

I challenged her: "So what do you get out of making them right?"

What's important to note about Rita's story is the way past

traumas such as being ridiculed and put down show up in the here and now as undisputed truths. Viral beliefs can convince us to act on assumptions that have no basis in reality and simply aren't true.

Rita agreed that she had not been able to separate fact from fiction. This recognition signaled me that she was ready to take the next step.

I asked her to check her beliefs against what is true for her now.

We listed verifiable facts:

- Rita graduated at the top of her class in business school.

- She is a leader in several prestigious organizations.

- She has never been skipped over for a promotion in her company.

- She has held and excelled (per performance reviews) in the executive role she has held for several years.

- Her net worth and annual salary exceed that of all five of her brothers.

- She is in a happy, stable marriage with her first and only husband, whereas her brothers have divorced at least once.

- She is a health enthusiast who stays in great shape and has run a marathon, while three of her brothers are very overweight and all five have a drinking problem.

Despite these verifiable, objective facts, Rita's subjective experience still tells her she is the lesser individual. And despite of or because of her success, her brothers are continually infuriated by her and go to great lengths to insult and criticize her just as they did when they were kids.

It was time for Rita to name her viral belief, disentangle her self-concept from this false belief, and put an end to her brothers' authority over her worth.

I had her say out loud her desire *and* her viral belief at the same time.

She stated, "I want to be a VP, but I don't think I'm smart enough."

Rita knew, intellectually, that this was not true, knew the belief did not reflect the reality of her value to the company as evidenced by every one of her performance reviews. Nonetheless, this erroneous belief had a life of its own.

We are all vulnerable to this type of unconscious, tenacious conviction, along with the companion "felt sense" and body language that match and reinforce the viral belief in the form of posture that still lived on in her body.

Returning to Rita, I instructed her to repeat "I want to be VP, but I don't think I'm smart enough" several times, moving the stuck energy out of her body. I suggested she tease apart her desire and her viral belief. This "teasing apart" can be quite a process, much like getting tangles out of a child's hair or untangling a fine chain that has knotted into a ball. It may require special tools, in this case keen awareness rather than a fine-tooth comb and scissors or needle-nose pliers. I instructed her to see these two threads and separate them, paying attention to the specific form they took—a thought, an emotion, a body sensation. I suggested she cut any strings she could not pull apart so that the two became distinct.

Then I said emphatically, speaking to both the adult Rita and the child whose self-concept had been negatively influenced by her siblings: "Your desire is real, but the belief you picked up from your brothers is a lie." As she worked inwardly to cut them apart, she visibly relaxed into herself.

Within a few moments, Rita began to laugh at the absurdity of her longstanding viral belief. She was ready to swap out that belief for a vital belief that matched her goal and reflected her accomplishments.

I had her reverse her viral belief by stating its opposite several times. She shouted, "I deserve to be a VP and am smart enough to step into the role."

She felt a little awkward at first. Her body didn't believe the words coming out of her mouth. I reassured her, explaining that it would take repetition and a period of time—as few as 30 days if she was consistent—to close the gap and embody her vital belief.

I gave her my favorite whole-body affirmation to take home with her: "I love, accept, and express myself as _____."

In Rita's case: "I love, accept, and express myself *as a smart woman who is VP-ready now.*"

A key to the power of vital beliefs is when your body, mind, and heart fall in love with the vision. This allows a deep integration that activates Whole Body Intelligence. From this alive place, we can clarify our purpose and take responsibility for our role in that mission. We jump in and express ourselves with new freedom and authenticity. This exponentially increases the possibility of actualizing the dream. Once you truly embody your vision and begin to act from that vibration, you will become a wildly powerful magnet for that which you desire.

Rita left the session renewed, confident, and excited to redo her résumé and apply for a VP position. Her "billboard" shifted dramatically. She walked out of my office with executive presence. She was now the person in mind *and* body who could step into the role of VP and succeed.

As she was leaving, she called out, "My vital belief makes me happy. I hear from everyone around me that I am ready to be a VP. Now I believe it too. By feeling it in my body, I now know that it is possible and time for me to rise to that position."

YOUR TURN: CHANGE A VIRAL BELIEF INTO A VITAL ONE

We are going to work with the body's energy system and cellular memories to correct the imbalances that hold on to self-sabotaging beliefs.

We'll work directly with cellular memories as they live in the body. As we've seen, beliefs that sabotage you don't just live deep in the folds of the brain where memory is stored. That's because the memory leads a sort of double life. On the one hand, it functions as a blockade, a "moat around your castle" that serves as a buffer zone or, in the psychological sense, a numbing mechanism. This keeps your viral beliefs activated in your subconscious all the time. Their job is to protect and defend you from further harm. On the other hand, memory can serve as an alarm system. When the red alert goes off, we experience a cascade of physical and emotional responses triggered by that memory. Both the blockade and the red alert confuse and distort your experience of the here and now.

Difficult, emotionally charged moments—traumatic, abusive, shameful, embarrassing, terrifying moments—are locked into the body. When we experience a similar situation or circumstance, neural circuits associated with the memory wake up. That neural circuitry and the chemical signals that travel along their paths are not isolated to your "memory banks"—they weave a web of unreality throughout the body.

The WBI belief process helps you access this web of information so you can:

- Recognize what has been running you from below the level of conscious awareness

- Become aware of physiological and emotional components of your viral beliefs

- Work with the beliefs where they live—in the body as well as the mind

- Clear outdated beliefs

- Install new ones

The WBI belief process employs many of the fundamental tenets and foundational techniques presented earlier in this

THE WBI BELIEF PROCESS

Phase 1

Make a commitment to give your all to this process. Shift your attention away from your external environment and toward your inner landscape. Stay attentive. Notice if your thoughts wander into the past or jump ahead to the future, and gently bring your attention to your breath. Scan your body. Report and adjust.

Phase 2

State your desire and then observe your body's response. Pay particular attention to your emotions and your body's sensations. What is your body saying to you about your desire? Notice any limited thoughts that reinforce your viral beliefs.

Phase 3

State your desire and report your body sensations. Say this out loud or to yourself:

"I want _____, *and* I notice _____."

Repeat, exaggerate, and shake out whatever energy your body wants to release. When you feel complete, become still.

Pay attention to memories or any images that arise. Do your best to disentangle your positive thoughts and feelings related to your desire from limiting thoughts and feelings linked to your viral belief.

Phase 4

State the opposite of your viral belief.

If your viral belief is "Success will make me sick," then your vital belief would be "Success will make me healthy."

Repeat your vital belief several times. Observe whether your body can absorb this new information yet. Repeat your vital belief often until your body adjusts and integrates it.

book, including breathing, scanning, reporting, moving, and expressing.

Like Rita, you will connect the dots from your past and release the numbing mechanisms that keep your viral beliefs stirring up trouble in your subconscious. Once you do this, you can finally dissolve unproductive beliefs and free yourself to achieve what you desire.

Each of the following phases is designed to help you identify and release viral beliefs so you can embody new vital ones.

Phase 1

Pause for a moment and make a commitment to give your all to this process. Shift your attention away from your external environment and toward your inner landscape. Stay attentive. Notice if your thoughts wander into the past or jump ahead to the future and gently bring your attention back to your breath.

Put all of your focus on your breath. What do you notice about your breathing pattern? Is your breath originating from your lower diaphragm or higher up in your chest? Is it easier to inhale or exhale? Does your breath seem to get stuck anywhere when you breathe in and out? Stay connected to your breathing. Slow down and simply observe.

Scan your body from head to toe. Report your observations, either subvocally or aloud. Notice all the sensations in any part of your body. Notice tension or tightness; tingling, vibrating, or twitching; pain or discomfort; a pleasant sense of relaxation; perhaps even hot or cold sensations. Then declare what you notice out loud. Describe each sensation. For example, "I notice anxiety in my chest or tingling in my arms."

When you are ready, say, aloud or to yourself, "I notice _____."

With your fingertips, touch the area where you feel this sensation. Breathe into these areas in your body. You might want to palpitate the area by tapping lightly, allowing that sensation to connect your brain and body. Do whatever helps you become keenly aware of what is happening for you in the moment.

At this point, take a minute or two to gather any important information that your body is offering you. How do you feel compared to when you began the process?

Phase 2

Next let's go deeper into your body to gather the information we need to identify your viral beliefs.

Take a moment and tune in to what you want in your life right now. You might wish to lose weight, fall in love, or have more freedom to travel.

Visualize yourself having what you want. Breathe in deeply through your nose and out through your mouth. As you inhale, use your imagination and breathe your desire in so that it fills your whole body. Feel your desire bathe every cell. Let your body fill up with the positive emotions associated with having what you want—excitement, joy, satisfaction, connection, happiness, peace.

State your desire with total conviction. Frame your statement this way: "I want _____" or "I desire _____."

Gather important information, emotions, and beliefs that arise in response to stating your desire. Let your body do whatever it wants in response to the information you gathered. If your fist wants to grip and punch a pillow, let it. If your arms want to rise in a big, happy yes, let them.

Phase 3

State your desire *and* report on your body sensations at the same time. Say them out loud or to yourself: "I want _____, and I notice _____."

Try it again: "I want _____, and I notice _____."

Repeat, exaggerate, and shake out any energy that your body wants to release.

Notice if a belief or memory arises as you do this.

If you identified a viral belief that has blocked your desire, name it: "My viral belief is _____."

Express everything you feel about that belief through your body. Use words, sounds, movements, shaking. Follow your body's lead. Don't hold back.

As you do this, open to feel and experience any familiar emotions or memories that surface. These may be linked to your desires or your beliefs. You may feel sadness or fear about not having your desire realized. You may feel anger when you identify the source of your block. Your goal is to excavate and disperse the energy held in your body by the viral belief.

If no memory arises, that's fine. In this phase of the process, you are releasing trapped energy whether or not you experience a memory or dramatic release. Acknowledge your gain, whatever it is. As you do the practice over time, your awareness will travel deeper into your subconscious and unconscious terrain.

Again state your desire and viral belief silently or out loud, this time with the intention of separating them: "I desire _____, and I notice _____ (viral belief)."

Do your best to disentangle positive thoughts and feelings related to your desire from thoughts and feelings wrapped up in your viral belief. This is how you stop your viral belief from overriding what you truly desire. Said another way: Once you disentangle your desire from your viral belief, your desire is free to manifest.

Phase 4

Now let's replace your viral belief with a vital one.

State your desire, and program your vital belief into your body-mind.

For example, many of us carry a viral belief that falling in love will lead to getting hurt. The vital belief to replace this with would be, Falling in love will bring me lasting love.

Repeat your vital belief several times. Notice how your body absorbs this new information. Repeat your vital belief again and again and again so it fully sinks in and embeds in your body and mind. Play with this; make it fun. Vital beliefs are a source of energy and joy. That's part of their healing magic.

Make an affirmation that you will use daily and often. To embody it even more, you'll begin with the phrase "I love myself as _____ (your vital belief)."

Touch your heart and say, "I love myself as _____."

Then touch your belly and say, "I accept myself as _____."

Next touch your throat and say, "I express myself as _____."

Now say all three together in one affirmation. "I love, accept, and express myself as _____."

For example, let's say your viral belief is "If I produce my music CD, no one will like it." The vital belief would be something like: "I love, accept, and express myself as a successful producer of music that people really like."

You can further simplify the belief. For example, let's say your viral belief is "If people hear my music, they won't like it." The vital belief would be: "I love, accept, and express myself as a musician, and people love my music."

Write out your affirmation, post it where you will see it, and embody it by speaking it out loud often.

You can be led through this process by listening to the audio version on the WBI Web site. Here's the link: WholeBodyIntelligenceBook.com/WBIBeliefProcess.

You now have a strong foundation in WBI and have developed the needed skill sets: the body-first approach, the rebooting technique, and the WBI belief process.

All the practices and insights you've gained will converge in the next chapter, where you will be introduced to a unique whole-body 30-day plan designed to retrain your subconscious mind so you can make positive changes that last.

PART IV

CREATE POSITIVE CHANGES THAT LAST

CHAPTER 9

THE WBI 30-DAY LIFESTYLE PLAN

CONGRATULATIONS FOR FOLLOWING THE map and taking your WBI journey this far. We started the journey by talking story and learning about Whole Body Intelligence. You learned foundational tenets and explored WBI tools to expand your perspective in any situation with the body-first approach. You discovered that body and movement awareness exercises have a positive impact on how you perceive and interact with the world. You gained understanding of the causes and conditions that contribute to physical stress, and you learned to manage stress with the rebooting technique (TRT). Then you faced old patterns and beliefs that were getting in your way and began to change them by infusing new patterns in your body-mind.

I've worked in the fields of success and wellness long enough to know better than to leave it at that. A crucial leg of the journey is still ahead. I promised to teach you how to be Whole Body Intelligent, to help you get out of your head and into your body so you can make positive changes that last.

Now it's time to do that. We're going to take everything you've learned and apply it in your life. You will start exactly where you are, and you will practice WBI as you go on a five-star thrill ride to bring your visions to life and fulfill your deepest desires.

This chapter provides you with a plan that will install Whole Body Intelligence into your subconscious mind and into your body at a cellular level. We want the work to sink in—to literally begin to form new grooves and pathways in your nervous system. When you follow the plan, limiting beliefs and the energy they hold can be dispersed. This allows new, vital energy to flow into your system as you form new beliefs and healthy patterns. In time the new will subsume the old and become dominant. This is how you bring about embodied change.

In Chapter 10 we will zero in on three traits that are key to successful completion of the 30-day plan and that keep you fresh and fired up. Develop these traits and you will build momentum as new attitudes and aligned actions become effortless. This is how to make changes that last.

WHY 30 DAYS?

When NASA did a test to see how much time was required for an astronaut to adapt to a new way of seeing things—literally—the agency found that it requires 25 to 30 days of daily mental retraining for the subconscious mind to accept new input as fact and for new habits to be neurologically ingrained in the body and mind.

The test tracked and measured astronauts to see how they responded to being upside down in space without gravity. The astronauts wore special convex lenses—goggles that made the world look upside down. They were required to wear the goggles 24/7 for 30 consecutive days.

Somewhere between days 25 and 30, every astronaut tested began to see the world right side up. Their brains had created fresh neural pathways that turned the inverted image 180 degrees so they would see as though they were not wearing the goggles. The human brain is that adaptable—over time.

When the astronauts removed their goggles, it likewise took their brains 25 to 30 days to readjust and see the world the right way up again.

NASA then did a second study. This time the astronauts removed their goggles for 24 hours on day 15, halfway through the experiment. The brains of those astronauts took a total of 40 to 45 days to flip the upside-down image to right side up. That one 24-hour hiatus interrupted the adaptation process completely. Remember that the next time you are tempted to cheat "just this once."

NASA concluded that it takes an uninterrupted period of up to 30 days to reprogram your unconscious mind and develop a new habit.

I encourage you to follow the program for 30 days in a row. If you can complete only two pages on the weekend for the next 15 weekends, this will still maximize your ability to form positive attitudes and habits by generating new neural pathways. If you aren't ready to commit for 30 days for any reason, then I suggest you read the section for day 1, where you will map out your intentions. This essential first step will assist you in drawing on all your energy to begin the program with articulated intent, total awareness, and an inspiring purpose. Your intention and purpose will keep you on track, moving in the direction you really want. The power of setting intentions, having a plan, and keeping your word by acting on your commitment gives you a rock-solid foundation from which to consciously create your life the way you desire it to be. The bonus is that you will feel happier and more joyous along the way.

PRACTICE MAKES PERFECT

Let's face it. At times we've failed to follow the plan or didn't practice enough to get what we wanted. I wanted to be a drummer, but my first teacher handed me a stick and a rubber block. Not fun. I wanted to rock out on a full trap set. I was told to practice every day until my next lesson. I didn't want to hit a rubber block. I wanted to sit at the trap set and try one tangible element of my dream. I wanted to feel the initial rush and excitement of hitting wood on the skin of the drums. My instructor had a different plan for me, one that he knew worked: practicing on a rubber block. I never went back.

We all have had other people's plans, agendas, and ideas foisted upon us. At times our parents or teachers gave us plans we either couldn't relate to or didn't want to follow. Following plans sometimes meant we had to join an organization or group that we didn't like. Or plans meant being forced to practice something like a piano every day, which wasn't as cool as hanging out with your friends after school.

To master any skill, you have to practice. You have to practice until the doing becomes automatic, instilled in muscle memory, and relatively effortless. I say *relatively* to highlight the importance of ongoing discipline, especially for complex tasks. When you perform an action or activity regularly, the electric signals in your brain fire in a regular pattern through strings of nerve cells that then clump together in a fairly set pattern. This process is called myelination, wherein the electrical signals that go through your brain become insulated by a sheath that surrounds the axon of a neuron. The axon is like a long, slender arm that conducts electricity from one neuron to the next. Repetition causes myelination, strengthening neural pathways. This is why a skier can take a variety of runs down the slope and feel a sense of mastery and exhilaration. He no longer has to pay attention to every shift of his weight and placement of his pole; his neurology literally does this for him. What's more, our brains love learning and love mastery all the more, thus we are rewarded for the work we've put in. Simply put: Mastery feels good.

At age 15 Jerry Garcia got his first guitar. By 1960 he was touring the world with the Grateful Dead. In 1986 Jerry collapsed into a diabetic coma that lasted for 5 days. The coma dramatically affected his basic motor skills. He had to completely relearn to play the guitar. Jerry practiced and practiced and practiced. He dedicated himself to a specific goal: to go back out on tour with his bands. By the end of the year, he was back onstage with the Dead and the Jerry Garcia Band.

You get the point. Get motivated, and you will follow a plan that's well worth following.

THE WBI 30-DAY LIFESTYLE PLAN FORMAT

On day 1 of the 30-day program, you will get in touch with your desires and the motivation behind them. Follow your plan and practice it every day for 30 days. You deserve to have the life you want.

Each day you will engage all of your intelligences: IQ (intellectual), EQ (emotional), and BQ (body). The plan is designed to facilitate inner shifts in awareness and perspective as you walk, talk, and work through your world. Each day has practical, goal-oriented action steps to produce significant positive results and changes in your life.

Over 30 days you will:

- Develop greater self-awareness and confidence

- Experience a noticeable change in your breathing and movement patterns and an increased sense of well-being

- Experience greater congruency and alignment between your conscious and subconscious feelings, beliefs, and actions, resulting in more authentic body language

- Access new levels of energy, optimism, and motivation relative to important inner and outer goals

- Enjoy improved personal and business relationships

- Form a healthier, honest relationship with yourself

Let's Keep It Simple

Plans with too many words, stories, and concepts can be hard to follow and take too much time. The 30-Day WBI Lifestyle

Plan gets right to the point and is user and time friendly so you can have a sense of accomplishment each day. With the plan you will receive:

- **A daily theme.** Revisit and practice material from the book.

- **A body-centric focus and exercise.** Stay engaged with the theme that day.

- **An evening inquiry.** Check in, reflect, and review at the end of each day. Log insights and results relative to the experiences produced from your daily activities.

- **Private links** for *Whole Body Intelligence* readers. Download themes and exercises onto your smartphone, tablet, or computer or print them out to post on your desk, daily task board, car dashboard, etc. Find these links at WholeBodyIntelligenceBook.com/30dayplan.

- **Support.** You can interact with other readers who are following the plan and share experiences with them on the community Web pages: WholeBodyIntelligence.com/Community.

Tips for a Successful Experience

Before you begin the 30-Day WBI Lifestyle Plan, I have important suggestions that can ensure a more enjoyable, successful experience:

- **Discern.** This plan is a private experience; you are learning about you.

It is wise to be selective and decide if you want to do the plan by yourself or with a partner, book club, or support group. Pick the best approach for you. Be around people who support your commitment to change and want this for you as much as you want this for yourself. All it takes is one negative comment from someone important to you to throw you off. Discern.

• **Start new.** As with all plans, it is best to begin with a fresh canvas.

Take a few moments now and decide what old stories you would like to leave behind over the next 30 days. Embark on the plan from a place of wonder and curiosity. Forgive yourself for past behaviors. Let go of disappointments and results that were unsatisfying. Up until now you have done your best. You've met innumerable challenges and landed on your feet. Congratulate yourself for arriving at this moment and start with a fresh slate. Leave the past behind.

• **Love yourself throughout.** Do your best to stay neutral and learn from every feeling, experience, and nugget of wisdom that comes your way during the 30-day plan. Watch out for the critical parent, brother, or competitor's voice inside that might pop in and judge you. This is not a pass-fail plan. It is a journey for you to enjoy, a time to learn more about yourself. You now know how to breathe and move through any uncomfortable feeling or memory that may surface. Love yourself every step along the way.

• **Set realistic goals.** I truly believe in unlimited possibilities and visions, so I absolutely want you to go for it. And yet I do want to remind you to notice every win and to build on those wins to reach for bigger goals. Think of a runner training for a marathon. To build her strength and endurance, she will start by running shorter distances and gradually increase the number of miles she puts in each week. Most marathon runners do not run 27 miles during their training period. They break up those miles into realistic distance runs every training day. Set goals that you believe you can take over the finish line.

Ready, get set, . . . GO.

DAY 1
┤ SETTING YOUR INTENTIONS ├

TODAY'S FOCUS

EXAMINE your life and your desires.

SET intentions that inspire purposeful action.

TODAY'S EXERCISE

SET at least one specific intention to actualize in the next 30 days. Make it concrete and measurable.

CLARIFY the motivation behind your intention. What tangible rewards do you desire?

WRITE your answers down and read them aloud. Notice how your body feels as you do.

END-OF-THE-DAY REFLECTION

How did today's focus and exercise affect my thinking?

_____

What emotions surfaced?

_____

What did my body tell me?

_____

DAY 2
{ BODY FIRST }

TODAY'S FOCUS

SHIFT your attention from your mind to your whole-body experience.

TODAY'S EXERCISE

IN at least three situations today (having lunch with a friend, walking alone in nature, sitting in a business meeting, driving the kids to school, and so on), consciously shift your attention from your mind and thoughts to your whole body, your visceral experience. Feel the whole experience your body is having during those situations. Observe, feel, listen, and learn.

END-OF-THE-DAY REFLECTION

How did today's focus and exercise affect my thinking?

_____

What emotions surfaced?

_____

What did my body tell me?

_____

DAY 3
·{ BREATH AWARENESS }·

TODAY'S FOCUS

STAY in touch with your breathing throughout the day and evening.

TODAY'S EXERCISE

TAKE hundreds of conscious breaths today. Visualize vital energy flowing into your body when you inhale, and then let any stress, agitation, or worry flow out of you on the exhalation.

AT least four times today, spot-check your breathing. Focus on where your inhalation originates. Are you taking full, deep breaths and expanding your belly, or are you breathing into your upper chest and using only the top of your lungs? Is your breath strained or labored on the inhale, or are you restricting or controlling the outflow of breath on the exhale? Simply observe. Let go of any judgments. Today is about finding your baseline. Observe, feel, listen, and learn.

END-OF-THE-DAY REFLECTION

How did today's focus and exercise affect my thinking?

_____

What emotions surfaced?

_____

What did my body tell me?

_____

DAY 4
⊰ BODY AWARENESS ⊱

TODAY'S FOCUS

GET in touch with your body as often as possible.

TODAY'S EXERCISE

THROUGHOUT the day and evening, bring your attention to your body and notice the full range of your somatic experience.

AT least four times today, take a break, unplug for 3 minutes, and get out of your head. Put 100 percent of your attention on your body. Do your best to put up a screen between you and the outer world.

BREATHE in and out consciously as you scan your entire body. Concentrate on what is happening internally. Start at the top of your scalp and go all the way down to your toes. Notice any sensations, any tension or gripping. Observe your posture and your stance. Is your weight squarely on both feet? Are your feet firmly on the ground? Is your posture contracted or expansive? What about your shoulders—are they relaxed or hunched up toward your ears? Each time you scan, make any adjustments that make you feel more relaxed and confident. Observe, feel, listen, and learn.

END-OF-THE-DAY REFLECTION

How did today's focus and exercise affect my thinking?

_____

What emotions surfaced?

_____

What did my body tell me?

_____

DAY 5
⁍{ MOVEMENT AWARENESS }⁌

TODAY'S FOCUS

STAY aware of how you move through life.

TODAY'S EXERCISE

STAY cognizant of your movements—both obvious and subtle—as much as you can throughout the day.

NOTICE the pace at which you move. Do you walk slowly, or do you tend to race around? Are your feet faced outward (1:05 and 1:55 on a clock) or straight ahead? Do you hold your head high, or are your eyes cast downward? Do you cross your legs every time you sit down? Do you stand still or shift your weight back and forth when you're waiting in line? Do you take long strides or short ones? Do you walk heel and toe, or do you tend to slide your feet?

BE especially aware of how you move when you transition: get into or out of a car, stand up or sit down at your desk, walk into or out of a room.

END-OF-THE-DAY REFLECTION

How did today's focus and exercise affect my thinking?

_____

What emotions surfaced?

_____

What did my body tell me?

_____

DAY 6
⋅{ YOUR BODY BILLBOARD }⋅

TODAY'S FOCUS

BECOME aware of the micromessages you communicate with your body.

TODAY'S EXERCISE

BECOME aware of the messages you send out. Be diligent. Catch subtle signals: physical gestures, facial expressions, and involuntary or habitual movements. Pay attention to the tone of your voice, the pacing of your speech, the volume at which you typically talk. What causes you to speak louder or softer? Faster or slower? Be honest with yourself: Are your words congruent with your body language?

END-OF-THE-DAY REFLECTION

How did today's focus and exercise affect my thinking?

_____

What emotions surfaced?

_____

What did my body tell me?

_____

DAY 7
⋅{ EXPANSION AND CONTRACTION }⋅

TODAY'S FOCUS

BECOME aware of fluctuations in your body.

TODAY'S EXERCISE

EITHER standing or sitting, open your body by moving it into a position that makes you feel bigger and more expansive. Take a mental photograph of that position. Experience how that feels. Next close your body by moving it into a position that makes you smaller and contracted. Take a mental photograph of it. Experience how that feels. Throughout this day, stay aware and notice when you expand and open in a power pose versus when you slip into a powerless pose. As Jean Shelton, the renowned method acting teacher, told me many times in class, "When there's a change, catch the beat."

END-OF-THE-DAY REFLECTION

How did today's focus and exercise affect my thinking?

_____

What emotions surfaced?

_____

What did my body tell me?

_____

DAY 8
┤ BODY APPRECIATION DAY ├

TODAY'S FOCUS

BE grateful for your body.

TODAY'S EXERCISE

THINK about someone you love unconditionally. It might be your cat, your child, or your grandmother. Next transfer that feeling of love to your body, your loyal ally who is there for you 24/7. Thank your body several times throughout the day. Tell your body you love it exactly as it is. Give love especially to the areas of your body that you tend to judge or feel embarrassed about. Thank the areas of your body that have taken punches or stored hurtful emotions. For instance, "I love my tummy and thighs and appreciate all that you have done and do for me." Acknowledge those body parts with your loving touch.

END-OF-THE-DAY REFLECTION

How did today's focus and exercise affect my thinking?

_____

What emotions surfaced?

_____

What did my body tell me?

_____

DAY 9
⁅ STRESS AWARENESS ⁆

TODAY'S FOCUS

NOTICE how you respond to stressors from the outside and inside.

TODAY'S EXERCISE

STAY aware of which external stimulus and/or internal thought triggers your stress response today.

NOTICE how your body responds to environmental conditions, people you interact with, and any specific stressful thoughts you have about your past or future.

MAKE a list of five or more specific stressors that trigger your anxiety, and indicate where you feel each response in your body.

END-OF-THE-DAY REFLECTION

How did today's focus and exercise affect my thinking?

_____

What emotions surfaced?

_____

What did my body tell me?

_____

DAY 10
⦗ STRESS AND FINANCES ⦘

TODAY'S FOCUS

EXPLORE the effect of your finances on your stress levels.

TODAY'S EXERCISE

TAKE inventory today.

HOW often are your personal finances on your mind?

WHAT emotions do you feel when you think about your finances?

ARE your purchases more impulsive than planned? If so, why?

WHAT messages did you learn about finances from your parents?

WHEN it comes to managing and planning your finances, what do you feel in your body?

DOES anything need to change about your relationship to your finances? If so, what action or actions will you take?

END-OF-THE-DAY REFLECTION

How did today's focus and exercise affect my thinking?

_____

What emotions surfaced?

_____

What did my body tell me?

_____

DAY 11
⁍{ STRESS AND RELATIONSHIPS }⁌

TODAY'S FOCUS

TAKE inventory of your relationships with people, paying particular attention to how relating to another affects your energy.

TODAY'S EXERCISE

ANSWER these questions. How often do you feel stressed over personal and business relationships? Does a difficult relationship stay on your mind even when you aren't interacting with that person? Make a list of five people with whom you have a strained relationship. What emotions and sensations do you feel when you think about these people?

RATE, using a scale of 1 to 10, the amount of stress you feel with each person on your first list. What, if anything, can you do to lower your stress? Do you need to contact them and state what you need, stop interacting with the person for a time, or let go of the relationship? Feel the effect on your body and take action.

END-OF-THE-DAY REFLECTION

How did today's focus and exercise affect my thinking?

What emotions surfaced?

What did my body tell me?

DAY 12
·{ STRESS AND WORK }·

TODAY'S FOCUS

STAY aware of what stresses you at work and explore what you can do to change that.

TODAY'S EXERCISE

WHETHER you work independently, work at an office, rear children at home, or do all of the above, make a list of specific stressors you typically encounter during the course of a day. Now list some of the atypical, unexpected, distracting, unpleasant stressors that have cropped up over the past several weeks. Notice your body's responses as you review these contributors to stress. What body sensations arise? What emotions? On a scale of 1 to 10, how much stress do you experience at work?

LOOK at any beliefs you might have about work. Are you hardwired to think of work as stressful? What is your attitude toward working most days? Identify any viral beliefs or counterproductive attitudes you have about your job. What specific action or actions can you take to make your work less stressful and more productive?

END-OF-THE-DAY REFLECTION

How did today's focus and exercise affect my thinking?

What emotions surfaced?

What did my body tell me?

DAY 13
{ YOUR STORY }

TODAY'S FOCUS

REWRITE old stories about yourself that don't reflect who you are now and who you want to be.

TODAY'S EXERCISE

REFLECT on your self-talk. Listen for story lines and tales (tall or otherwise) you identify with. What kind of impact do your stories have on others? For example, your story may say that you are too overweight to launch a singing career. Your story may say that you are too flawed to fall in love.

ALL of these negative stories stem from viral beliefs. Today, dedicate yourself to identifying any limiting stories you tell yourself and/or others over and over. Feel the impact they have on your body as you identify them. Rewrite each story in light of who you are today and who you ultimately would like to be. For instance, "I am the perfect size to launch my singing career." Or "I have grown into a person who knows how to be in a loving relationship." Then notice how the new story feels in your body. Beginning today, stop telling the old stories and tell only the new ones. This process has a huge effect on self-image, productivity, and outcomes.

END-OF-THE-DAY REFLECTION

How did today's focus and exercise affect my thinking?

_____

What emotions surfaced?

_____

What did my body tell me?

_____

DAY 14
{ REBOOTING }

TODAY'S FOCUS

ENJOY the benefits of taking time to recharge on a regular basis by using the rebooting technique (TRT) three or four times.

TODAY'S EXERCISE

MAKE at least three appointments with yourself today. Set aside 5 to 7 minutes to practice TRT. Put the appointments on your calendar and set the alarm on your smartphone so you don't forget. Follow the steps in Chapter 6 or listen to the audio instruction found at WholeBodyIntelligenceBook.com/TRT. Do your first session at the start of your day to set the right tone for the exercise. Book the other two or three appointments any time during the day or evening.

END-OF-THE-DAY REFLECTION

How did today's focus and exercise affect my thinking?

_____

What emotions surfaced?

_____

What did my body tell me?

_____

DAY 15
{ BREATH AWARENESS }

TODAY'S FOCUS

STAY engaged with your breathing throughout the day and evening.

TODAY'S EXERCISE

BREATHE consciously and take special note of any improvements in your breathing since you began your WBI 30-day plan. Take hundreds of conscious breaths today.

VISUALIZE vital energy flowing into your body when you inhale, and then let any stress, agitation, or worry flow out of you on the exhalation.

AT least four times during the day, pause and spot-check your breathing. Notice where your inhalation originates. Are you taking in full, deep breaths and expanding your belly, or are you breathing into your upper chest and using only the top of your lungs? Simply observe. Let go of any judgments. Notice if your breath is strained or labored on the inhale, or if you are restricting or controlling the outflow of breath on the exhale. Observe, feel, listen, and learn.

END-OF-THE-DAY REFLECTION

How did today's focus and exercise affect my thinking?

_____

What emotions surfaced?

_____

What did my body tell me?

_____

DAY 16
{ BODY AWARENESS }

TODAY'S FOCUS

STAY engaged with your whole-body experience throughout the day.

TODAY'S EXERCISE

TAKE a deep breath and notice if you feel more connected to your body now compared to when you started this plan. At least four times, unplug for 3 minutes and get out of your head. Do your best to put up a screen between you and the outer world. Put 100 percent of your attention on your body. Breathe in and out consciously as you scan your body. Concentrate on what is happening internally.

START at the top of your scalp and go all the way down to your toes. Notice any sensations, any tension or gripping. Observe your posture and your stance. Is your weight squarely on both feet? Are your feet firmly on the ground? Is your posture contracted or expansive? What about your shoulders—are they relaxed or hunched up toward your ears? Each time you scan, adjust your body so you feel more relaxed and confident. Observe, feel, listen, and learn.

END-OF-THE-DAY REFLECTION

How did today's focus and exercise affect my thinking?

_____

What emotions surfaced?

_____

What did my body tell me?

_____

DAY 17
{ MOVEMENT AWARENESS }

TODAY'S FOCUS

STAY aware of how you move your body.

TODAY'S EXERCISE

TAKE a deep breath and notice if you feel more aware of how you move through life now compared to when you started this plan. Stay especially aware of how you move your body in different situations.

NOTICE the pace at which you move. Do you hold your head high, or are your eyes cast downward? Do you cross your legs every time you sit down? Do you take long strides or short ones? Do you walk heel and toe, or do you tend to slide your feet? Notice any idiosyncratic movement patterns.

BE especially aware of how you move when you transition from one activity or position to another and how you walk into or out of a room.

END-OF-THE-DAY REFLECTION

How did today's focus and exercise affect my thinking?

_____

What emotions surfaced?

_____

What did my body tell me?

_____

DAY 18
┧ BELIEFS ┣

TODAY'S FOCUS

IDENTIFY and rewrite any beliefs that may be sabotaging your life.

TODAY'S EXERCISE

BY now you have a sense of the core beliefs that color the way you see the world. Today you will write down one pesky, tenacious belief that you would like to change. Next identify where that belief came from. Spend some time and review your thoughts and behaviors related to that belief to determine if it's still operating in your life. Imagine if that belief were totally cleared and released. What would change in your life? How might you feel in your body? Are you ready to let that belief go? If so, set some time aside today to review Chapter 8, or listen to the audio instruction found at WholeBodyIntelligenceBook.com/WBIBeliefsProcess. It's time to bust that viral belief once and for all.

END-OF-THE-DAY REFLECTION

How did today's focus and exercise affect my thinking?

_____

What emotions surfaced?

_____

What did my body tell me?

_____

DAY 19
{ BELIEFS ABOUT SUCCESS }

TODAY'S FOCUS

EXPLORE your specific beliefs about success and any feelings you experience in your body about having it.

TODAY'S EXERCISE

HOW often is success or the lack of it on your mind? How do you define success for yourself? What emotions arise when you think about success? What messages did you learn about success from your parents?

WRITE down any beliefs about becoming more successful than you are today. Is that belief driving you toward or away from success? Does it influence how you approach or avoid new situations and challenges? Do you believe that by changing that belief you will be open to more success? If so, what action or actions will you take to change it?

END-OF-THE-DAY REFLECTION

How did today's focus and exercise affect my thinking?

_____

What emotions surfaced?

_____

What did my body tell me?

_____

DAY 20
{ BELIEFS ABOUT LOVE }

TODAY'S FOCUS

EXPLORE your relationship to love and any beliefs you have about getting more of it in your life.

TODAY'S EXERCISE

HOW often is love on your mind? What emotions arise when you think about having more love? What messages did you receive about love from your parents?

TODAY write down one belief you have about your love life. How does that feel in your body? Is that belief drawing love toward you? Repelling love? Does the belief affect how attractive you feel and/or your willingness to meet someone new or break through to new heights with your present partner? Do you believe that changing your belief will bring more love? If so, what action or actions will you take to change the belief?

END-OF-THE-DAY REFLECTION

How did today's focus and exercise affect my thinking?

_____

What emotions surfaced?

_____

What did my body tell me?

_____

DAY 21
·{ ROMANTIC NOTIONS }·

TODAY'S FOCUS

LOOK squarely at ideas or misconceptions that misdirect your energy or keep you stuck.

TODAY'S EXERCISE

BE real with yourself and flush out any romantic notions you have about yourself, about others, about endeavors or situations that no longer serve your best interests. For instance, we might hold on to thoughts like "I realize it's been 10 years of abuse, but I remember how sweet he used to be. He'll be like that again," or "My best friend in college used to be so much fun to hang out with, but I can't stand being around her now. I keep trying, hoping she will be fun again one day." List one or two romantic notions you have about yourself or another or about a situation you are dealing with. Sometimes facing reality and letting go of past but no-longer-true vignettes will free you to fill your life with new and real outcomes.

END-OF-THE-DAY REFLECTION

How did today's focus and exercise affect my thinking?

_____

What emotions surfaced?

_____

What did my body tell me?

_____

DAY 22
⊰ WHOLE-BODY COMMUNICATION ⊱

TODAY'S FOCUS

BE aware of how you communicate.

TODAY'S EXERCISE

STAY aware of what your body is telling you when communicating with others by phone, e-mail, and text or in person.

IN every communication you have today, stay aware of what your body is saying. For instance, you might notice your stomach tightens when you're talking with someone who's dominating the conversation and won't let you get a word in. You might discover that you bounce your leg up and down ever so slightly or speak rapidly when trying to close a sale. Let your body in on your conversations today.

NOTICE if you are really engaged, making eye contact, and listening intently to other people or if you're thinking about something else while interacting with others.

END-OF-THE-DAY REFLECTION

How did today's focus and exercise affect my thinking?

_____

What emotions surfaced?

_____

What did my body tell me?

_____

DAY 23
·{ BREATH AWARENESS }·

TODAY'S FOCUS

STAY engaged with your breathing throughout the day and evening.

TODAY'S EXERCISE

BREATHE consciously and evaluate any improvements in your breathing since you started the program. Take hundreds of conscious breaths throughout the day.

VISUALIZE vital energy flowing into your body when you inhale, and then let any stress, agitation, or worry flow out of you on the exhalation.

AT least four times during the day, pause and spot-check your breathing. Notice where your inhalation originates. Are you taking in full, deep breaths and expanding your belly, or are you breathing into your upper chest and using only the top third of your lungs? Simply observe. Let go of any judgments. Notice if your breath is strained or labored on the inhale, or if you are restricting or controlling the outflow of breath on the exhale. Observe, feel, listen, and learn.

END-OF-THE-DAY REFLECTION

How did today's focus and exercise affect my thinking?

_____

What emotions surfaced?

_____

What did my body tell me?

_____

DAY 24
{ BODY AWARENESS }

TODAY'S FOCUS

STAY engaged with your whole-body experience throughout the day.

TODAY'S EXERCISE

TAKE a deep breath and notice if you feel more connected to your body experience than you did 8 days ago when you last experienced a body awareness day. At least four times today, unplug for 3 minutes and get out of your head. Put 100 percent of your attention on your body. Breathe in and out consciously as you scan your body. Concentrate on what is happening internally. Start at the top of your scalp and go all the way down to your toes. Notice any sensations, tension, or gripping. Observe your posture and your stance. Is your weight squarely on both feet? Are your feet firmly on the ground? Is your posture contracted or expansive? What about your shoulders—are they relaxed or hunched up toward your ears? Each time you scan, make adjustments so you feel more relaxed and confident. Observe, feel, listen, and learn.

END-OF-THE-DAY REFLECTION

How did today's focus and exercise affect my thinking?

What emotions surfaced?

What did my body tell me?

DAY 25
·{ MOVEMENT AWARENESS }·

TODAY'S FOCUS

STAY aware of how you move your body.

TODAY'S EXERCISE

TAKE a deep breath and notice if you feel more aware of how you move through life compared to when you started the WBI program.

SPEND the day investigating and learning about how you move in different situations: while interacting with people, in relationship to time, when you shift from one activity to another. Even if you have to rush to an appointment, stay aware of how you move your body during that transition. Is there anything more you want to learn about yourself in relationship to how you move?

END-OF-THE-DAY REFLECTION

How did today's focus and exercise affect my thinking?

_____

What emotions surfaced?

_____

What did my body tell me?

_____

DAY 26
{ BREAKING THE CHAIN }

TODAY'S FOCUS

UNCOVER any hand-me-down cultural or familial beliefs, traits, or patterns that you'd like to modify or release.

TODAY'S EXERCISE

WRITE down at least one or two viral beliefs handed down from family, coaches, teachers, or anyone else in authority. List at least one or two negative habits or behaviors you adopted because of (or to rebel against) these beliefs. As you read what you have written, stay aware of changes in your mood and your energy level. Observe any thoughts, rationalizations, excuses, or frustrations that relate to these hand-me-down beliefs. Consider if you have passed these beliefs on to your children, partners, coworkers, or loved ones. Use the WBI belief process discussed in Chapter 8 to remove these beliefs from your body and break the chain.

NOW formulate a vital belief and go out and model that.

END-OF-THE-DAY REFLECTION

How did today's focus and exercise affect my thinking?

What emotions surfaced?

What did my body tell me?

DAY 27
·{ WHOLE-BODY WELLNESS }·

TODAY'S FOCUS

DEVELOP a plan to maintain optimal health.

TODAY'S EXERCISE

DEFINE where you are now vis-à-vis your health. Take a stand for where you want to be healthwise. Gather all the information and insight you've gained over the past 26 days. Now it's time to design a personal wellness plan.

WRITE down any changes you would like to make in your diet. Notice how your body feels as you do that. Write down any regular exercise you would like to add to your existing routine. Be specific. If you don't exercise, name one activity you will start doing today and, at minimum, 4 days a week going forward. It can be as simple as a 12-minute walk or 20 pushups and 20 situps. The key is to up your commitment to self-care and be good to your body.

ARE you drinking enough water? Do you want to add supplements, superfood drinks, or herbs to your regimen? What action or actions will you take on behalf of your health today?

END OF DAY REFLECTION

How did today's focus and exercise affect my thinking?

What emotions surfaced?

What did my body tell me?

DAY 28
∙{ PASSION AND PURPOSE }∙

TODAY'S FOCUS

ALLOW your life's purpose to inspire everything you do.

TODAY'S EXERCISE

AS you move through your day, maintain an awareness of your higher purpose. Consider the following questions: What is the purpose of my life right now? What inspires me to do the things I do? What gifts do I have to share that energize me and serve others?

AT the end of the exercise, answer this question: What actions can I take now to ignite my purpose and allow it to galvanize, uplift, and bring joy into all areas of my life?

END-OF-THE-DAY REFLECTION

How did today's focus and exercise affect my thinking?

What emotions surfaced?

What did my body tell me?

DAY 29
⊰ COMMUNITY ⊱

TODAY'S FOCUS

EXPLORE how to bring your purpose, vision, and gifts to your community.

TODAY'S EXERCISE

ASK yourself if you are satisfied with the amount of connection you have with those in your community. Remember Blue Zones people and the way their lives revolve around community. How might you tap into the community or communities in your vicinity or even online? Do you have interests that you can share and enjoy with others? What about a runners' club? A cooking class? A business networking group or book club? Are you interested in local government or professional associations? Are you a current member of a group that you could up your participation in? What about forming a Meetup group around your interests? Or perhaps you might start writing a blog.

END-OF-THE-DAY REFLECTION

How did today's focus and exercise affect my thinking?

What emotions surfaced?

What did my body tell me?

DAY 30
{ EXAMINE AND RESET YOUR INTENTIONS }

TODAY'S FOCUS

LOOK back at the intentions you set 30 days ago and consider your next plan of action.

TODAY'S EXERCISE

REVIEW the intention you set on day 1 of your 30-day WBI lifestyle upgrade. Notice how you feel about your results. Did you meet or exceed your expectations and hopes? Breathe and shake out any feelings that arise.

NOW set at least one specific goal—with a date of completion—for each of these areas of your life: health, career, relationships, finances, personal and spiritual growth.

CLEARLY articulate the motivation that drives each new goal.

READ each goal out loud and notice how your body feels.

END-OF-THE-DAY REFLECTION

How did today's focus and exercise affect my thinking?

What emotions surfaced?

What did my body tell me?

CHAPTER 10

STAY ENGAGED AND PURPOSEFUL—NO MATTER WHAT!

WORLD SERIES CHAMPION RYAN Vogelsong, nicknamed "Vogey," had dreamed of pitching in the World Series since he was a boy. Shortly after the San Francisco Giants won the pennant, I heard an interview with Vogey on local talk radio. He told the show's host about a conversation he'd had with his wife a few weeks earlier. He admitted having complained to her that their friends didn't seem happy about their lives and weren't "as much fun as they used to be."

His wife's reply took him by surprise. She said, "Ryan, not everyone gets to live out childhood dreams like you did and still do." Vogelsong got it. Since that day, he's had far more compassion for people who aren't living their dreams, and he feels deeply grateful for the life he has achieved.

When the host asked Vogey how he'd created his "field of dreams" life, he answered without hesitation: "I never lost faith in my dream." From the time he was a young boy, little Ryan had a dream that he would one day pitch in the World Series. He believed in his dream so much that he never wavered in the face of the many challenges that came his way. He bounced back from pitching slumps where he had strings of losses. No matter what happened, he kept his eye on his promise to himself: to do whatever it takes to get to the Big Show. What a thrill and how surreal that moment must have been for him the first time he walked onto the pitcher's mound in a World Series game.

There are as many ways to achieve success as there are people who have done so. Peak moments leave you with the feeling that you have arrived. There is no happiness quite like what comes with actualizing a dream that was born as a belief, a gut sense, or a vision. Vogey's reflections on his success reinforced what I know to be true about realizing dreams: Reaching a goal boils down to three essentials: staying *engaged*, building *resilience*, and embodying your *purpose* from head to toe.

Engagement. Resilience. Purpose. These qualities are the key to mastery. They give you a springboard to maintaining a high level of awareness and well-being on the way to realizing your dreams. Moreover, these are the traits you must bring to bear to create the positive changes you desire and to have them last.

We've all had the experience of setting a firm resolution to reach a goal or fulfill our desires only to lose our initial enthusiasm. Without that euphoric rush, the resolve required to succeed becomes elusive. What happens to the sense of conviction to stay the course and the certainty that this time it will stick?

Ideas and inspirations come from our essence, from the core of who we are, yet many of us have an overlay of subconscious fear and doubt that stops us from acting on those ideas and inspirations. Sometimes when our dreams start coming true—when we land a great job, sign a recording contract, or meet our soul mate—the feelings of excitement are accompanied by discomfort because we're in unknown territory. Often the mere act of stepping into exciting new terrain brings inactive viral beliefs to life.

You'll know a viral belief has come into play if you are swarmed by the feeling "I don't deserve this" or the premonition that "Something bad will happen if I go down that path." This is why some wins—and some relationships—are short-lived.

Subconscious subterfuge prevents us from enjoying the win over the long term. Most of the time, we aren't aware that we are undermining ourselves. For instance, a man might spend thousands of dollars on a matchmaking service or hundreds of hours on Internet dating sites to finally meet the woman of his dreams and then suddenly push her away. Or a woman may work overtime and bust her chops to get a promotion then forget a critical deadline, get dinged in her next performance review, and subsequently get passed over for promotion. There is no logical or rational explanation why the man's behavior would suddenly belie his intent to form a lifelong partnership. The woman has no history of missing deadlines, much less forgetting that a project is due, and yet she is certain she never saw the memo. What is going on?

The tricky part is that we can't always put our finger on what's going on. This paradoxical phenomenon is so common that we have graphic idioms that sum it up in powerful images such as "she shot herself in the foot" or "he had just enough rope to hang himself."

It's true: There is no rational explanation for this all-too-common psychological pickle. The causal factors—unconscious beliefs, deeply buried memories, habitual tensions, and energy blocks held in the body—speak louder than reason and, at times, work in direct opposition to our stated desires.

The man will of course attempt to explain his behavior to his ladylove. The woman will likely redouble her efforts to prove her competence to her supervisors. But pushing away and missed deadlines are only symptoms. Here's the real issue: The ability to stay engaged and on purpose has been subverted by an irrational gestalt that lives in the body and mind. This gestalt acts like a kind of "set point" that influences, and sometimes outright governs, behavior. It goes something like this: Your body is accustomed to a certain level of joy and life satisfaction. When you actualize your desire, or when a goal is within reach, your body experiences a large influx of positive energy. This energy rushes through your body, and your system cannot assimilate it.

It's a bit like having a thermostat that measures pleasure and success. Your body is accustomed to a familiar level of energy that keeps you comfortable. We adjust when we're unhappy or dissatisfied by turning up the heat and pushing ourselves to do better. We likewise adjust when we get too happy or have more success than usual by turning the heat down and slacking off or subverting ourselves in some way. Bottom line: We will do whatever it takes to return to the cozy place we know so well.

We see a perfect example of this syndrome in reports of lottery winners who take home megamillions but squander their winnings, ruin their marriages, or become ill not long after they collect their prizes.

The National Endowment for Financial Education points to research that estimates 70 percent of people who come into large sums of money without working for it lose it within 7 years. Lottery winners and trust fund recipients who lost their fortunes often attempt to explain it away—the money was lost due to poor investment advice, a fall in the markets, or other circumstances beyond their control. What they do not address is the underlying driver that sent them in a misguided direction in the first place: the limiting beliefs that live in their body.

Here's my take on it. A man is unhappy with his financial situation. He's angry with himself, angry at his friends who are more well-off than he, angry at the economy, the government, the banks, the crooks on Wall Street; you name it. He identifies with this angry stance and is accustomed to grumbling and ranting about it, both in his mind and in his conversations with others. He's actually quite comfortable complaining about "the 1 percent" and feels a rush of righteousness when he gets beefed up about it. He wears a familiar scowl on his face whenever he thinks or talks about fiscal matters.

Then he wins the lottery. He's an overnight multimillionaire. It's a dream come true. But the change is too sudden, the exhilarating feelings too intense. He now has more choices than he has ever had before, but he does not choose wisely. Rather, he starts to blow the money in an unconscious effort to return to his comfort zone. His money thermostat is set for angry. His financial identity demands that he wear a scowl. Within a year, maybe two, his financial situation has reverted to where he started—or worse.

I imagine you are thinking, "Not me, I would never do

that." And you most likely wouldn't—yet it happens. Whether we desire more love, more money, more power, or more accolades, it happens.

Again and again I've seen people in my trainings light up and stand tall when they declare a dream or intention to the group, only to contract moments later. Their mind and even their emotions are invested in the dream, but their body isn't ready to carry that dream into reality. That rift is obvious in their body. It's as if they are carrying a sign with bold letters that announces: "Don't give me what I want, I can't handle it."

Self-sabotage sets up a tug-of-war between your desires and your actions. It's an unconscious process—until it's not. Once you realize that you are, in fact, undermining yourself, you can begin to break free by taking full responsibility for your behavior and your failures.

Whole Body Intelligence can alert you before you take an action that will disrupt your progress or diminish your ability to hold on to what you've already achieved. Now that you have developed a keen sense of what is happening in your body, this awareness can help you maintain positive energy and forward momentum. Moreover, you are now in a position to notice when you are about to sabotage yourself, stop, reboot, and prevent the old story from playing out again.

That's where staying engaged, resilient, and on purpose comes in.

Let's look at the interplay and influence each of these qualities has on the other.

To stay resilient and on purpose, you must be engaged with your whole body and your beliefs so you can stay in touch with what's really going on and not sabotage your progress.

You also need to be fully engaged with your feelings, alert to limited thinking or fearful scenarios generated by the mind that have little or nothing to do with what's actually happening over the course of a day.

Being on purpose keeps you engaged with yourself and others. Being on purpose is a fantastic motivator that compels you to take better care of yourself and get even better at what you do. Purpose breeds excellence. Purpose will inspire you to engage with others who are aligned with your purpose. Many of our most treasured friendships and fruitful partnerships are formed because we share a common purpose.

Purpose is like bounce-back insurance. Just when you're about to quit, when you feel defeated and totally tapped out, purpose will galvanize unforeseen resources. And then resilience will give you the courage to put those resources to work and engagement will show you your next best move.

Embody these three essential processes and you will be attentive and energized, clear on your priorities, attuned to your objectives, and keenly aware of the slightest hint of self-sabotage.

STAYING ENGAGED

The most precious gift we can offer
anyone is our attention.

—THICH NHAT HANH

Recently I received an invitation to a birthday party. The invite had the tagline "Please don't bring presents. Your presence is a gift." Sounds so easy, doesn't it? Just show up and be present. I wish it could be that easy. As human beings we possess a unique and powerful ability to focus our attention on the present moment and simply *be with* whatever is before us—a rose, a loved one, a business problem. We've all had the experience of getting absorbed when our attention is so focused, so singular, that we forget ourselves. The separate self is subsumed in the object of our attention. However, the brilliant human mind also has the ability to focus on events, people, concerns, etc., that are not right in front of us in the moment. We get pulled into the past or future. This ability is essential for planning the future or sorting through the past to share, celebrate, compare, reminisce, evaluate, understand, and many other cognitive functions—including learning from the past to avoid making the same mistakes.

This dual function is most certainly a benefit, but it can work to our detriment. If we are not discerning about how we direct and discipline the miracle of mind, if we let it wander too much, ruminate, or get too imaginative or too lazy, the mind can lead us to make bad decisions, insult or disappoint another person, and neglect or even hurt our body. At some point most of us eventually realize that our mind has gone off the rails or down a dead end and we bring ourselves back. Sometimes we wake up with a snap. Sometimes we stop gnawing on whatever we've been chewing too late and find that we've missed our exit on the freeway or stood up a friend we were scheduled to meet for lunch. The solution is to exercise presence on an ongoing basis, to stay engaged with the here and now.

This is exactly what you've practiced in this book and

anchored in your body and mind over 30 days. You've experienced the value of getting out of your head and into your body. If you take this up as a regular practice, you will stay present and have the needed attention not only to accomplish your goals but to enjoy the little moments in time along the way. Of course you will continue to drift off on occasion, likely daily. What will be different going forward is a new, exciting engagement with your body. This ability will become an asset. You will have the skill to steer your attention back to the present and focus on what's most important and most real.

A client summed this up when he admitted, "I'm sitting in a meeting, or watching my kid play in a Little League game, but I'm not really there. My mind is so wrapped up in who knows what that I am completely zoned out and out of touch with what's right in front of me. Sometimes I feel like the walking dead."

The dictionary defines the act of engaging as *holding attention* or *participating with*. But when the mind is overactive (or underactive, for that matter), it's just plain hard to engage and rein in our attention.

Anderson Cooper did a *60 Minutes* segment on this common problem in December 2014. The segment was called "Mindfulness." Cooper had attended a mindfulness retreat led by Jon Kabat-Zinn, PhD, a professor of medicine and the founder of the Center for Mindfulness in Medicine at the University of Massachusetts Medical School. Cooper was skeptical when he learned that the program involved little more than sitting, eating, and walking silently around the retreat center grounds.

But he was on a quest. He wanted to learn how to calm the monkey mind, how to slip into the quietude in the midst of a fast-paced world.

Cooper was a fast learner. It didn't take him long to realize that the ball was in his court. Dr. Kabat-Zinn had defined mindfulness as "the awareness that arises *on purpose* in the present moment." That means that it was up to him to purposely select the present and engage with whatever he was doing—eating or walking or listening to Dr. Kabat-Zinn.

Anderson Cooper spoke for many of his viewers when he admitted, "I am never present. Every moment I'm either thinking of something coming down the road or thinking of something that happened in the past."

He's not alone. We have slowly but surely given up or been conditioned out of full engagement with the present. Some of us are more involved with our smartphones than with real, live, flesh-and-blood people. And when the mind is hyperstimulated, it seeks more stimulation. Too often our addiction to technology steers us toward devices and distractions rather than people or important tasks at hand.

No doubt you can relate. Who hasn't sat at their desk working on the computer while their mind wanders off, perhaps planning a summer vacation, or considering restaurant options for dinner, or worrying about the kids, the remodel, the dentist bills—the list is endless.

According to researcher Matt Killingsworth, PhD, this makes us unhappy campers.

Dr. Killingsworth designs studies that gather data on happiness. While doing his doctoral research with Daniel Gilbert at Harvard, he invented a nifty tool for investigating happiness: an iPhone app that captured feelings in real time. (Basically, it pings you at random times and asks: How are you feeling right now, and what are you doing?) Data captured from the study became the landmark paper "A Wandering Mind Is an Unhappy Mind."

The focus of his app and research came from people's responses to three questions. The first was a happiness question: *How do you feel?* on a scale ranging from very bad to very good. Second, an activity question: *What are you doing?* on a list of 22 different activities, including things like eating and working and watching TV. And finally a mind-wandering question: *Are you thinking about something other than what you're currently doing?* People could say no (in other words, they are focused only on their current activity) or yes (they are thinking about something else). He also asked if the topic of those thoughts is pleasant, neutral, or unpleasant. Any of those yes responses are what he called mind wandering.

He collected 650,000 real-time reports from more than 15,000 people ages 18 to the late eighties in a wide range of incomes, education levels, marital statuses, and so on. The participants collectively represented every one of 86 occupational categories and hailed from 80-plus countries.

What did he find? First of all, that people's minds wander a lot. Forty-seven percent of the time, people are thinking about something other than what they're currently doing.

People were mind wandering at least 30 percent of the time. He determined that this pervades everything we do, that people are substantially less happy when their minds are wandering than when they're not, and that people are less happy when they're mind wandering no matter what they're doing.

As I stated earlier, I'm not suggesting that we can or want to stop mind wandering altogether, because at times going in the past and imagining the future is useful, but Dr. Killingsworth's results suggest that mind wandering less often could substantially improve the quality of our lives.

So like Dr. Kabat-Zinn suggested, remember to pay attention intentionally; that is, "on purpose." Engage and stay engaged as much as possible so you stress less and realize the results you desire more easefully and productively.

Take a moment and ask yourself:

How often do I stay present and engaged in the moment with my friends, family, and work?_____

_____

Do I engage less with my friends, family, and work than I used to?

_____

_____

If so, how committed am I now to changing that by using my whole body's intelligence to stay more attentive and aware in any situation? _____

_____

STAYING RESILIENT

Les Brown is a motivational speaker like no other and one of my personal favorites. The author of *It's Not Over Until You Win* and *Live Your Dreams,* he is a former member of the

Ohio House of Representatives and a former TV host. He is known for his phrase "It's possible," and his life is a testament to exactly that.

Brown grew up with his twin brother, Wesley, in an abandoned building. He was given up for adoption and then raised by a 38-year-old single woman who worked two jobs to make ends meet. He stuttered and was declared "mentally retarded" in grade school. To say the least, he did not do well—that is, until he was encouraged by an angel of a teacher to take a speech class. Brown's life changed from that class. He gained confidence and went on to learn everything he could to fulfill his potential.

Whenever I hear Les tell how motivated he was to turn his life around ("I was so hawwwwngry, I turned my setbacks into setups for success"), I think about resilience. He tells story after story about how he bounced back from adversity, of the divorce with Gladys Knight, of his struggle with a life-threatening illness that struck him later in life. Les Brown is a model of resilience.

Another speaker I admire is Kyle Maynard, an author, entrepreneur, and supreme athlete. I'm moved to tears when I see him speak. Kyle was born with a birth defect; his arms ended at the elbows, his legs near the knees. Yet nothing got in his way. He began to wrestle at age 11, set multiple weight-lifting records, fought in martial arts tournaments, played football (he said he was a fierce tackler), and most recently became the first man to crawl the entire route to the summit of Mount Kilimanjaro. Kyle overcame obstacles that most people would have viewed as insurmountable.

With the full support of his parents, at a young age Kyle embarked on a remarkable "pursuit of normalcy." That's been his attitude since. He types up to 50 words per minute on a normal keyboard using only his elbows. He eats and writes without any adaptations, drives a vehicle that has little modification, and lives on his own in a three-story townhouse in Atlanta. For me Kyle Maynard is my greatest teacher of resilience.

In both cases, Les's and Kyle's, we get a clear idea of what resilience is. Resilience refers to an individual's tendency to cope effectively with challenges, to courageously face adversity and bounce back to a previous level of functioning or to one better.

In cases where it may not be possible to neutralize a challenge entirely (as in the case of a tsunami or other natural disaster), resilience can still help you with damage control and get you on the path to rebuild and rebound. Whether we're faced with psychological, social, cultural, or physical challenges, resilience is the key.

We've seen that engaging requires shifting your attention and adapting to the adverse situation. Similarly, resilience requires directing your attention effectively too by doing whatever is necessary to neutralize the challenge or threat, like Les Brown and Kyle Maynard did.

Whole Body Intelligence and Resilience

Whole Body Intelligence gives you a leg up when you come upon an obstruction that gets in your way. Rather than letting your mind get snared by stories that tell you what you can and can't do, or just quitting, with Whole Body Intelligence you instead become resilient by engaging your body, by taking deep breaths, and by gathering a fresh perspective and new solutions that can help you overcome anything.

Resilience also requires changing viral beliefs into vital beliefs. Whole Body Intelligence can help you there too. Once you've uninstalled the viral belief and installed a vital one, it becomes easier to adapt and bounce back. You can then see your way clear to repair a broken relationship, reenergize a floundering project, and help your dreams spring back to life.

From a whole-body perspective, resilience means getting up from your desk when the inspiration starts to fail. When ideas aren't flowing easily or your back hurts, you can choose to take a walk or employ a mindfulness practice, like the rebooting technique.

From reading this book, you now possess the key to resilience. You know how to engage with your body-mind and shift, by choice, into a new state or another activity that "feels" like the next best move, to come back to a renewed, refreshed, and stronger you.

Resilience applies to every aspect of your life. You never know what will come your way, but if you know how to be resilient, then you can surf over almost any tough wave and land on your feet.

How You Build Resilience Is a Personal Choice

To get more insights on how resilience works, I contacted four leaders I respect and value: one each in business, psychology, movement therapy, and neuromuscular reprogramming. I asked them to define resilience from their perspective and to share what they do personally to get out of a funk or a stuck place and arrive somewhere better. Since I do work with their organizations, I am aware of how this topic is central for them now.

Christine Landon is the senior director of leadership effectiveness at Workday. Highly respected in her field, Christine is also one of the organizers of the Bay Area Executive Development Network, a Silicon Valley organization formed to advance the skills and knowledge of practitioners in leadership development. Christine knows how much resilience is needed in the workplace today. In her new position and in prior ones with large organizations like PayPal and Agilent Technologies, Christine emphasized that resilience must be learned and applied in our work, with our families, and to our overall personal well-being.

To Christine, resilience is "the ability to navigate nonstop change, and to quickly adapt to a changing environment in the external marketplace, in your family, and in your workplace." She adds, "It's a given that we're going to be ever evolving, so we need to have the ability to adapt and thrive in an ever-changing environment. Resilience is becoming vital, and differentiates those who can lead through the changes versus those who will be left behind." Christine sees resilience as a muscle that we need to intentionally work. "You need to develop that part of you so you can get better at handling change quickly and continually learning how to adapt and make good choices."

To build that muscle, she takes regular breaks and uses the

rebooting technique, meditation, and short walks outside during those breaks. Because of the amount of e-mails, meetings, multiple devices, and sudden changes in her work, she needs to break away and reflect, breathe, and listen to her body. Often on those short breaks, she asks herself, "Am I going to be able to lead myself through this, or is this a decision point for me to do something different?" What a brilliant question to ask! Like Christine, we each need to learn tools and activities that work for us and then take the best from each of them and create our own rituals for being resilient in today's fast-moving world.

Gay Hendricks, PhD, is a bestselling author, psychologist, and one of the most insightful people I know. Along with his wife, Dr. Kathlyn Hendricks, he founded the Hendricks Institute. Together they have authored more than 39 books.

When I asked Gay about his take on resilience, he immediately replied, "I see acquiring more resilience as a lifelong process." Then he went on to explain, "My daughter used to have this clown when she was little, about as tall as her with a weight on the bottom, and if she knocked it over it would come right back up. Life is partially a process of learning how to do that, because you're always going to be knocked around by things, whether it's emotional or just the circumstances of life. Learning how to come back from it is key.

"For instance, if you go on a diet or an exercise program, you might fall off; everybody does. The really important thing is your recommitment. It's the returning and the recommitting to your goal, your life journey, that's the important thing. We need to learn about recommitment because that's really, as I see it, the key to resilience."

When I asked Gay what he was doing nowadays to continue to build resilience, he got excited. "I go to the gym 3 days a week to work out with a trainer for 4 or 5 hours, and it's been life changing for me. I've redesigned my body and lost 40 pounds in the process and built my body into something that resembles more of an athlete than a paunchy self-help book writer." (I forgot to add that Gay is also one of the funniest men I know.) "I'm very dedicated to going to the gym, and I mention that because I am building resilience through riding my bike, going to the gym, and meditating. My goal is always to do things that soothe my nervous system and make it like Teflon."

Kathlyn Hendricks holds a doctorate in transpersonal psychology; she has been a board-certified dance/movement therapist of the American Dance Therapy Association since 1975. As one of my primary movement therapy mentors, she has helped me learn a great deal about how I move through the world. Because of the great contribution she has made to me and, as a result, to this work, I asked her to share her take on resilience.

This is what the brilliant mind-body educator had to say:

> To me resilience comes from movement and being creative, since both open new pathways in the brain. I make it a point to always be moving and keeping some flow of movement going through my body. Even as I'm talking to you now, I'm moving around. Resilience comes from contacting that flow of aliveness and flow of creativity and letting ourselves really experience that. I think one of the biggest issues that's really prevalent in our society

is people have gotten more heady and more disembodied. Yet we are resilient. I think that's partly why movement practices, dance raves, and flash mobs happen spontaneously in places like New York's Grand Central Station. There's an inherent need that humans have to move, to be resilient. It's how we've communicated with each other since the beginning of time.

Katie's personal commitment to building resilience includes bracketing her day with meditation, movement, and creativity.

I believe the more scheduled you are, the more you need a type of spiritual cleanser every day. Something to kind of erase grit and give you a sense of the clear space in your body. And there is an interesting thing that tends to happen out of that choice: Everything else seems to go much more easily. On occasions when I have not done that, or went unconscious, the "stuff" just seemed to pile up and there was never enough time for it.

When you are just sitting and thinking about something, you use a very small part of your brain. But when you move, you activate all parts of your brain. So the more that you move, particularly spontaneous movement or moving from your impulse, you're able to listen to different parts of your body. Then you can follow those impulses with a stretch or a wiggle or a bounce up and down.

Katie made one more great point that really landed for me:

Movement keeps you inner directed rather than outer directed. You're able to create your own authentic center rather than be tuned to what's trendy or what's going to get you approval or getting involved in competition with people—all outer-directed things that keep you from being resilient. Unfortunately the central issue of our times is that we move too often from fear and reactivity. The only way you can genuinely respond to life is when you're free from fear.

Jocelyn Olivier is the founder and director of the Alive & Well! Institute of Conscious BodyWork and the Healus Neuro Rehab Center in Marin County, California. Olivier founded the Association for Humanistic Psychology somatics program in 1990 and has dedicated 39 years to developing and refining Conscious BodyWork and neuromuscular reprogramming.

Olivier says the key to the door of healing is finding resilience. She clarifies the meaning and experience of resilience beautifully:

> With respect to the body, resilience has to include the idea of elasticity and bounce, the ability to bounce back. Resilience is found in the ability to surrender to your nervous system and physically release both the memory and the tension from past negative experiences.

She emphasizes the physiological reality of resilience.

> Your breath is the gear shift between the sympathetic and parasympathetic sides of your autonomic nervous system. Breathing shifts us into the parasympathetic system, where all healing takes place. The ability to move freely between sympathetic arousal and parasympathetic release, to me, is resilience.

Shock, emotional trauma, and physical accidents freeze us in a defensive stance physically and emotionally. The stasis of fright and freeze leads to suppression and constant tension. Constant tension results in lack of resilience and elasticity in body tissue, which inhibit circulation and cellular metabolism. Sympathetic hyperarousal is not a sustainable lifestyle. It does not allow us to rest and restore resilience in the system, so we don't heal from past trauma and stress.

To keep her body resilient, Olivier practices healthy breathing, coordination exercises, and WBI techniques to let go. She says, "My goal is to cultivate trust in my body's intelligence and to release the effort of using all of my life force to hang on to the mechanisms I adopted in the past for my survival. Resilience to me is that moment when I surrender and I feel alive."

How Will You Build Resilience?

As you can see, there are many ways to build resilience.

For me, when I come upon a challenge, small or large, I put my attention on my body. I use the rebooting technique, or jump on my mini-trampoline, or go up the road to the nearby eucalyptus grove and walk the trail with my chest open, listening to the sounds of nature and staying present with my breath. I write a lot, and my go-to for inspiration is getting my head underwater. (Nope, I don't have a waterproof tablet or smartphone; in fact, I make it a point to leave them behind when I head for the swimming pool or the ocean.) Submerging my whole body in water has never failed to unleash my creativity when I run out of ideas. Once my head goes under, my mind quiets, my body relaxes, and my creative intelligence starts to percolate new ideas and solutions. My body and mind have become so accustomed to this prescription for writer's block that my creative side is unlocked within seconds after I get into water. A new pathway opens. Repetition has built a solid bridge between the creative part of my brain and the physical experience of my body-mind hitting the water.

My fiancé, Amanda, has her unique method too. Along with TRT, yoga, and other exercises, whenever she feels overwhelmed she does a visualization she calls "the French Press." She uses this technique as an effective tool for "pressing out" overwhelming and negative energy. She named the technique after the French press method for making coffee, which uses a pistonlike mechanism to force ground coffee through hot water, sending the spent grounds to the bottom of the pot and leaving a full-bodied brew on top. When Amanda hits her limit, she sits quietly and visualizes herself like a French press, squeezing all of her tension and stress from previous interactions out of her system. She starts at the crown of her head and moves her energy, like coffee grounds in the carafe, down to her toes. She continues to visualize moving all unwanted energy out of her body. Within moments she is renewed, and, in her words, "back to my original essence." I can tell you it works. Instead of telling me about the stress she is experiencing, she quietly goes into her office, brews an imaginary cup of java, and drains it through the press until she is refreshed. In every case she walks out feeling much better. That's resilience.

Design your own resilience plan.

On a scale from 1 to 10, how resilient do you think you are when it comes to bouncing back from stress, challenges, or adversity?

_____

_____

What method do you use to bounce back now?_____

_____

If you don't have a method, what will you commit to in order to build resilience?_____

_____

STAYING ON PURPOSE

For me purpose ties everything together. Whatever your dreams and goals, when you have a sense of purpose fueling you, everyday challenges will strengthen rather than drain you. Purpose is the driver that keeps me engaged and resilient. Without purpose, I wouldn't be inspired to stay on track and realize my goals and dreams. Whether I'm facing a small task or a life-changing opportunity, taking a moment to ask myself this one question—"What is the purpose of what I am doing right now?"—produces a buoyant feeling in my body that helps me keep going. And when my body feels that resilience, my mind relaxes and I can reengage with whatever is in front of me and stay present. When I am on purpose, I make better decisions, I'm more effective, and, most of all, I get to feel real satisfaction. In short, having a purpose transforms my every endeavor by infusing it with meaning.

Taking the time to check in and ask *why* you are doing *what* you are doing builds determination. Ryan Vogelsong, Les Brown, and Kyle Maynard wouldn't be where they are today if they weren't driven by purpose.

One of my passions in life is helping individuals and organizations define their purpose and make sure that what they do day to day (whether in the trenches or soaring high) is in alignment with that purpose. Too much time and energy get wasted by wandering thoughts and limiting beliefs. Purpose is the thread that weaves through everything you do and provides you with the resilience to go forward. Studies have shown that people who live with a sense of purpose are happier and live longer.

My message is simple but potent: Bring purpose into everything you do, no matter how small or large. It will enrich every moment of your life.

CONCLUSION

YOU ARE THE LOTTERY

WE LOVE PRIZES. SWEEPSTAKES, lotteries, blue ribbons at state fairs, trophies from our bowling league, you name it. We also love to watch championships and award shows: the Super Bowl, the Olympics, the Oscars, the Grammys, the Golden Globes. In recent years, talent contests and survival challenges have proliferated: *American Idol, Dancing with the Stars, America's Got Talent, The Voice, Survivor.* It would take too many pages to list them all. Tens of billions of dollars are spent every year on our attempts to come out on top and take home the gold.

For spectators it's a way to step out of life as we know it and indulge the dream of coming out on top, beating the odds. The lottery brings the fantasy of winning the gold into our homes. "What would I do if tomorrow I won $30 million? If I just pick the right six numbers, my life will change completely. I can buy a gorgeous house and any kind of car I want."

We buy that ticket, or a dozen of them, even though the odds are ridiculous. The odds of winning the Powerball lottery, for instance, are 1 in 175.2 million. Stats show you're more likely to die from a bee sting (1 in 6.1 million) or be struck by lightning (1 in 3 million) than become a Powerball multimillionaire. But we turn away from the almost near-impossible mathematical odds and buy the ticket anyway.

Like the trademarked lottery slogan goes, "Hey, you never know."

It doesn't faze us. We know it's a game. We like the game because it gives us hope, and hope is a feel-good thing. And there's something magical about the process. We allow ourselves to think that maybe, just maybe, we will defy the odds and be the one who wins.

One day I was talking about this with a group of people in a Whole Body Intelligence training. The conversation had come around to a discussion about prizewinners who find a way to sabotage their good fortune, when a strange feeling came over me. I felt tightness in my chest, noticed it, and continued my talk.

After the session I went upstairs to my hotel room, put my hand on my chest, and breathed in and out. I realized that a part of me had gotten activated by the conversation about prizes and lotteries, how much we want them, and how readily people sabotage themselves. I thought about what I wanted at the time, and two things flashed up immediately: I wanted to meet my beloved, and I wanted to sell my first solo book to a New York publisher. As I acknowledged that, I felt my chest open up. I kept declaring out loud what I wanted and had an epiphany.

I wanted to win the lottery, except the jackpot for me was to fall in love and get published. What came to me was profound. I thought, "Instead of longing for these, what might happen if I actually saw myself as the prize, the jackpot? How might that affect the chances of my having what I want?" I stood up, walked over to the mirror, and said out loud: "I am the lottery. I am the prize." I said it several times in a row and made a commitment to not just think or visualize it but actually embody the feeling inside of me that I *am* the prize and I *am* the lottery.

After a few weeks of doing this, I saw a distinct change in my feelings about and around women. My confidence grew from the inside out and I began to believe that, to a woman, I was a real catch. "I can be a great partner to play, love, and grow with," I thought to myself.

Then I did the same regarding a book publisher, thinking, "The publisher who signs me will get a great book and a skilled marketer to promote that book."

I kept repeating this affirmation for about 3 months. I would not only say it, I would feel it and breathe it into my body. My confidence was at an all-time high. It wasn't long before I met Amanda, whom I am engaged to and have enjoyed partnership with for 8 years. A few months later, I signed a book publishing deal for *What's Your Body Telling You?* To this day, whenever I get low or lack confidence, I say, "I am the lottery." I breathe that in and out, and I feel better.

My friend, as our journey together concludes, I have a message from the deepest source of my heart for you.

YOU are the lottery.

Try it.

Say it to yourself several times: "I am the lottery."

Breathe that in, feel how that feels.

Blessings on your journey.

RESOURCES FOR STAYING WHOLE BODY INTELLIGENT

Subscribe to Steve's e-letter

Receive a free body intelligent kit with guided meditations, interviews, and stress management tools. Plus, receive biweekly articles, blogs, Mindful Moment videos, and more!

wholebodyintelligence.com/subscribe

Enjoy a complimentary BQ (Body Intelligence) Audit

Assess and learn more about your breathing patterns, body awareness, self-talk, and more.

wholebodyintelligence.com/bq_assessment

Experience WBI with Steve by phone or Skype

wholebodyintelligence.com/coaching#program1

Make big leaps in your life in a private 2-day intensive with Steve

wholebodyintelligence.com/coaching#program2

Partner in a 6-Month Mentorship Program with Steve

Steve mentors a handful of people annually. Apply to bust through limiting beliefs and have a no-holding-back cheerleader in your corner and the ultimate accountability coach for achieving your goals and dream projects.

wholebodyintelligence.com/mentor

Join Steve on an adventure/training in Maui, Hawaii

wholebodyintelligence.com

Train to be a WBI coach

Build a Whole Body Intelligence coaching career.

wholebodyintelligence.com/coaching#program5

Change Your Beliefs, Change Your Mind

Four instantly downloadable videos where Steve helps you discover, release, and change limiting beliefs

wholebodyintelligence.com/beliefs

Boosting Your Personal and Professional Mojo

Ten instantly downloadable audio lessons and meditations with Steve, plus worksheets

wholebodyintelligence.com/mojo-onedream

Follow Steve on Facebook

facebook.com/SteveSisgold

Follow Steve on Twitter

@Sisgold

Enjoy Steve's YouTube channel

SteveSisgoldTV.com

Read Steve's blog library

wholebodyintelligence.com/blogs

Additional Resources

Lissa Rankin's prescriptions for healthy living
LissaRankin.com

Preventive Medical Center of Marin
An integrated medicine healthcare facility

pmcmarin.com

Center for Integrative Medicine
A WBI-focused medical practice

kaycorpusmd.com

Intuition Medicine phone sessions and women's gatherings
relaxandbefree.com

Optimal Breathing Mastery Kit
Optimalbreather.com

Nia, a cardio-dance workout and movement practice
nianow.com

INDEX

Underscored page references indicate sidebars and tables.
Boldface page references indicate photographs.

A

Abuse, 84, 103, 175
Adjusting, step 5 of reboot, 140
Adrenaline, 136
Affirmations
    audio version of WBI for, 194, 219,
        223
    new beliefs and, 76
    phase 4 of WBI and, 193–94
    to realize dreams, 263
    tension release and, 64
    for viral beliefs, 186
Aging, stress and, 100
Altered state of mind, 22–23
Anger, 75, 102–6
Animals, stress response in, 100–101
Anxiety
    fear and, 107–8
    old beliefs and, 61–64, 150–51
    physical symptoms and, 158
    technology and, 113–14
Attention
    body-first approach and, 3–18
        advantages of, 8
        children and, 9–10, 13–14
        focusing on one thing, 7–9
        habits and, 15–18
        mind, denying body, 10–12
    choice of where to place, 18
    outward and inward, 126–28
    relationships and, 125–26
    shifting, 3–6, 53–54, 156, 207
    wandering mind, 9, 238, 242–48
Audio instructions for Whole Body
        Intelligence, 194, 219,
        223

Autobiography, movement, 67–89
    advantage of, 88–89
    beneficial movement patterns,
        85–86
    group exercise, 81–85
    high-impact events, memories of,
        86–88
    memories and, 67–76
    parents, influence of, 76–79
    writing exercise, 79–81
Autonomic nervous system, 134
Awareness of body, 51–65. *See also*
        Movement autobiography
    anxiety and, 61–64
    body language, 36, 154, 185, 211
    brain and, 52–55
    emotions, understanding through,
        57–61
    expansive movements, 55–57, 212
    resilience and, 254–56
    stress and, 55–57
    WBI Lifestyle Plan and, 207,
        209–11, 221–22, 229–30

B

Babies. *See* Children
Back health, 118–20
Balance, stress and, 134
Behavior
    executive presence and, 58–61
    mimicking parents, 76–85
    mood and, 55–57
Beliefs. *See also* Viral beliefs
    anxiety and, 61–64, 150–51
    environment, effect of, 174–77

Beliefs (*cont.*)
    limiting effect of (*see* Trauma,
      effect of)
    of love, 225
    rewriting, 223, 231
    self-sabotaging, 239–42
    of success, 224
    vital, 154–55
Belly breathing, 62, 138
Beta state, 77
Blood pressure, 137
Blue Zones, 98–99, 116
Body, awareness of, 51–65. *See also*
    Movement autobiography
    anxiety and, 61–64
    body language, 36, 154, 185, 211
    brain and, 52–55
    emotions, understanding through,
      57–61
    expansive movements, 55–57,
      212
    resilience and, 254–56
    stress and, 55–57
    WBI Lifestyle Plan and, 207,
      209–11, 221–22, 229–30
Body cues
    adjusting because of, 51
    during communication, 154, 227
    examples, 40–41
    stress and, 110–11
    viral beliefs and, 153–54
Body-first approach, 3–18
    advantages of, 8
    children and, 9–10, 13–14
    exercises to shift attention, 4–7
    focusing on one thing, 7–9
    habits and, 15–18
    mind, denying body, 10–12
Body language
    awareness of, 8
    professional interactions and, 36
    social media and, 117–18
    viral beliefs and, 154, 185
    WBI Lifestyle Plan and, 211, 227
Brain
    adaptability of, 198–99
    attention and, 127
    body movement awareness and,
      52–55
    of children, development of, 77
    do-overs and, 70–71

    emotions and, 57–61
    habits and, 15
    practice and, 201
    stress and, 103, 107–8
Breakdowns, from stress, 101–3
Breathing
    awareness of, 208, 220, 228
    from belly, 62, 138
    children and, 33–34
    exercises for, 40
    exhale, difficulty with, 159,
      179–80
    for phases of WBI, 191–92
    posture and, 118
    repressed emotion and, 161–62
    resilience and, 256–57
    shallow, 61
    to shift attention, 5
    step 2 of reboot, 137–38
Bullying, 104–6
Burnout, 111–12

C
Celebrations of Life event, 21–22
Cell phones, 111, 115–19, 203. *See*
    also Technology
Cellular damage, stress and, 100
Cellular memory, emotions and,
    157–63, 167, 187–88
Centenarians, 98
Chakras, 27
Change, adapting to, 238, 242–43,
    248–57
Childbirth, 32–33
Children
    belief systems of, 174–77
    body-first approach and, 9–14
    development of, 77
    education of, 12
    genetics and, 173–74
    learning from, 32–34
    mimicking adults, 76–85
    parents' disapproval of, 60–61,
      73–76
    parents, influence of, 12–14,
      47–48, 167, 174–77
    siblings and, 180–82
    technology and, 115–18,
      124–25
Chronic pain, 157–66

Chronic stress, 102, 138. *See also* Stress
Comfort zones, 240–41
Communication
  body language and
    awareness of, <u>8</u>
    professional interactions and, 36
    social media and, 117–18
    viral beliefs and, 154, 185
    WBI Lifestyle Plan and, 211, 227
  children, belief systems of, 174–77
  love
    finding, 193, 262–63
    of oneself, 204, 213
    parents' disapproval of children,
      60–61, 73–76
Community, connecting with, 234
Complaining, 241
Computers and technology
  addiction to, 124–25
  distraction of, 14, 246
  posture and, 118–20
  rebooting computers, 128–30
  stress and, 99, 111–15, 121
Confidence, 36, 58–61, 159, 263
Consciousness movement, 34
Coping skills, 102–4
Core strength, 119
Cortisol, 108, 136
Creativity, 257–58

D

Danger, perception of, 99–100,
    106–8, 124–25
Decision-making, 11, 18
Defense mechanisms, 74
Denial of body, 10–11
Depression, 119–20, 172
Desires, stating, 191–93. *See also*
    Affirmations
Diet, 98, 232
Digestive problems, 119
Digestive system, mind of, 172
Distractions, 14, 136–37, 246
DNA, 173
Do-overs, neural pathways and,
    70–71, 74–76
Doubt, of dreams, 238–39
Downloads for WBI, 203
Dreams, realizing, 43, 237–43

E

Eastern philosophy, 26–27, 172
Embodied cognition, 3, 9–10, 18
Emotions. *See also* Stress
  body movement and, 57–61, 69–71
  cellular memory and, 157–63, 167,
    187–88
  exploring (*see* Movement
    autobiography)
  gut response to, 172
  habits and, 15–17
  physical healing and, 163–67
  physical reactions to, 16–17,
    45–46, 158–67
  repressing, 61–64, 152, 155,
    157–63
Energy
  meditation and, 26–27
  movement and, 56
Engagement, mindful, 238, 242–48
Enteric nervous system, 172
Environment
  adapting to, 252
  beliefs, effect on, 174–77
  cells, effect on, 174
  stress and, 214
Evolution, 118, 124–25
Executive presence, 58–61
Exercise for health
  importance of, 98
  posture and, 119–20
  resilience and, 254
  technology and, 118
  for wellness plan, 232
Exercises, WBI
  group
    movement autobiography, 81–85
    movement awareness, 58–61
    for stress release, 95–96
  to shift attention, 4–7
  writing
    for beliefs, rewriting, 223, 231
    history, rewriting, 70–71, 74–76,
     218
    parents, influence of, 79–81
    for resilience, 259
    for staying engaged, 248
    viral beliefs, recognizing, 168–69
    for WBI Lifestyle Plan, 206–35
Expansive movements, 55–57, 212
Exteroception, 127

F

Facial expressions. *See* Body language
Family dynamics
   children mimicking adults, 76–85
   communication, cell phones and,
      115–16
   parents' disapproval of children,
      60–61, 73–76
   parents' influence and, 12–14,
      47–48, 167, 174–77
   siblings and, 180–82
Farm (commune), 33
Fear
   defensiveness and, 257
   dream realization and, 238–39
   financial, 148–50
   of loss, 61–64
   mimicking parents, 87–88
   stress and, 100, 106–8
Feldenkrais Method, 42
Fight-or-flight response, 61, 100,
      133–34
Financial difficulties, 147–50, 215,
      240–41
Focusing on one thing, 7–9
Free will, 3–4, 9, 11

G

Games, electronic, 115–18
Garcia, Jerry, 201
General adaptation syndrome, 110
Genetic expression, 173–74
Glen Ivy, California, 38
Goals, 205, 235. *See also* Intentions
Gratitude, 213
Gravitas, 58
Group exercises
   movement autobiography, 81–85
   movement awareness, 58–61
   for stress release, 95–96
Gut, mind of, 172

H

Habits, 15–18, 198–200, 231
Happiness, 55–57, 126, 246–48
Harmony, inner, 27
Headaches, 119–20
Health, maintaining, 232

Heart disease, 119–20
Heart rate, stress and, 122–23, 123,
      136–37
Heredity, 173–74
Heroes, mimicking, 78–79
High-impact events, 68–69, 86–88
History
   reenacting, 68, 71
   rewriting, 70–71, 74–76, 218
Holocaust, 43–46
Hope, 262
Hormones
   body movement and, 55
   imbalances of, 137
   stress and, 107–8, 113, 136–37
Humiliation, effect of, 69–71, 75
Hurrying, 81–85

I

Identity
   memories as, 104
   of nerve cells, 54
Ikaria, Greece, 98
Illness and disease, 106–9
Immune system, 141
Indian philosophy, 27
Inflammation, 119, 141
Inner landscape, 23
Inner peace, 126
Instagram, 117
Instincts, 8
Integral Yoga, 27
Integrative medicine, 164
Intentions
   group exercise for, 95
   for reboot, 141–42
   for WBI Lifestyle Plan, 199–200,
      206, 235
Interoception, 127–28
Inward attention, 126–28

J

Joint health, 118–20
Judgment of others, 138

K

Kundalini, 26

L

Lamaze method, 32–33
Late arrival, fear of, 83–85
Leadership, 58–61
Lifestyle Plan, 197–235
    brain adaptability and, 198–200
    format of, 202–3
    practice, importance of, 200–201
    30-day plan, 206–35
    tips for, 203–5
Limbic bridge, 127
Limiting beliefs, 218. *See also*
        Trauma, effect of
Listening skills, 36
Living in the moment, 28–30, 97–98
Longevity, 98
Loss, fear of, 63–64
Lottery winners, 240–41, 261–62
Love
    beliefs of, 225
    finding, 193, 262–63
    of oneself, 204, 213
Lung capacity, 118
Lymph flow, 119

M

Meditation
    chakras, focusing on, 27
    rebooting technique (TRT) as, 133
    Transcendental, 133
    types of, 24–25
Memories
    cellular, emotion and, 157–63, 167,
        187–88
    embedding in body, 152–55
    limiting beliefs and (*see* Viral
        beliefs)
    movement autobiography for,
        67–89
        advantage of, 88–89
        beneficial movement patterns,
            85–86
        group exercise, 81–85
        high-impact events, memories of,
            86–88
        memories and, 67–76
        parents, influence of, 76–79
        writing exercise, 79–81
    old beliefs and, 150–52

phase 3 of WBI and, 192–93
physical healing and, 163–66
"poor person" mentality, 147–50
recalling, body movement for, 69–70
stress and, 103–6, 108, 119
viral and vital beliefs and, 153–56,
    175–77
Mental clarity, 111–13
Mental cognition, 3, 9
Mental regressions, 68
Mental retraining. *See* Whole Body
        Intelligence (WBI) Lifestyle
        Plan
Micromessages, 36
Mind
    altered state of, 22–23
    body movement and, 52–55
    denying body, 10–12
    of gut, 172
    quieting, 6, 127–28
    wandering, 9, 238, 242–48
Mindfulness, 245–46
Mind-over-body rule, 11–12
Mobile phones, 111, 115–19, 203. *See
    also* Technology
Mood, movement and, 55–57
Motivation, 201, 249
Motivational speakers, 248–50
Movement autobiography, 67–89
    advantage of, 88–89
    beneficial movement patterns, 85–86
    group exercise, 81–85
    high-impact events, memories of,
        86–88
    memories and, 67–76
    parents, influence of, 76–79
    writing exercise, 79–81
Movement of body, 51–65
    anxiety and, 61–64
    awareness of, 52–55 (*see also*
        Movement autobiography)
    body language, 36, 154, 185, 211
    emotions, understanding through,
        57–61
    expansive movements, 55–57, 212
    Lifestyle Plan and, 207, 209–11,
        221–22, 229–30
    resilience and, 254–56
    stress and, 55–57
Movement regressions, 71, 74–76

Multitasking, 111–13
Myelination, 201

N

Neck and back health, 118–20
Negative energy, 174
Negative thoughts, 8. *See also* Viral
    beliefs
Nervous system
    enteric, 172
    parasympathetic, 133–35, 256
    sympathetic, 61, 133–35, 256–57
Networking, 38–39
Neural nets, 54
Neural pathways
    adaptations and, 199
    do-overs and, 70
    new, growing, 53–55
    practice and, 201
Neurological problems, 119–20
Neuromuscular movement education,
    41
Neuronal synapses, 108
Neuroplasticity, 54–55
Nicoya peninsula, Costa Rica, 98
Nonverbal messages
    awareness of, 8
    professional interactions and, 36
    social media and, 117–18
    viral beliefs and, 154, 185
    WBI Lifestyle Plan and, 211, 227

O

Observing, step 3 of reboot, 138–39
Ogliastra, Sardinia, 98
Okinawa, Japan, 98
Outward attention, 126–28
Overthinking, 127–28

P

Paper tiger phenomenon, 106–8,
    124–25
Parasympathetic nervous system,
    133–35, 256
Parents
    disapproval of children, 60–61,
        73–76
    genetics and, 173–74

influencing children, 12–14, 47–48,
    167, 174–77
mimicking of, 76–85
Past. *See also* Memories
    letting go of, 204, 226
    reenacting, 68, 71
    rewriting, 70–71, 74–76, 218
Patterns of movement. *See* Movement
    autobiography
Phases of Whole Body Intelligence,
    190–94
Photo albums, 117–18
Physical abuse, 84
Physical contact, 117–18
Physical fitness
    importance of, 98
    posture and, 119–20
    resilience and, 254
    technology and, 118
    for wellness plan, 232
Physical reactions to emotions, 16–17,
    45–46, 158–67
Physical response to stress, 99–101,
    106–8
Physiological cycle of stress, 110–11
"Poor person" mentality, 147–50
Positive energy, 174, 240
Posture, 118–20, 139–40, 185
Power posing, 55–57, 212
Practice, 54, 200–201
Problem solving, 52–55, 133
Public speaking, 30–31, 67–68
Puerto Vallarta, Mexico, 93–99
Purposeful action
    after reboot, 141–42
    goals and, 238
    importance of, 242–43, 259–60
    Lifestyle Plan and, 233–34

R

Radiance Breathwork, 42–43
Rationality and reason, 11
Rebooting technique (TRT), 121–43
    attention and, 125–28
    benefit of, 132–33
    daily practice of, 133
    effectiveness of, 121–23, 142
    evolution and, 124–25
    heart rate and, 122–23
    importance of, 108–9

nervous system and, 133–35
online resources for, 142
practicing, 219
rebooting, defined, 128–31
step 1: unplug, 135–37
step 2: breathe, 137–38
step 3: observe, 138–39
step 4: report, 139
step 5: adjust, 140
step 6: visualize, 140–41
step 7: reboot, 141–42
step-by-step, overview, 135, <u>143</u>
Recommitment, resilience and, 253
Regression, 68, 71, 74–76
Relational intelligence, 117–18
Relationships
    attention and, 125–26
    family (see Family dynamics)
    romantic, 193, 262–63
    stress and, 216
    viral beliefs and, 154
Reporting
    phase 3 of WBI, 192
    step 4 of reboot, 139
Resilience, 238, 242–43, 248–57
Respiration. See Breathing
Road rage, 102
Romantic notions, 226
Routine patterns, 15–18

S

Sabotaging beliefs, 239–42
Sadness, repressed, 62–63
School shootings, 101–2
Self-assessment. See Movement
    autobiography
Self-awareness, 36
Self-consciousness, 150–51
Self-talk, 218
Senses, 9–10, 126–27, 137–39
Serotonin, 157
Shaktipat, 26, 38–39
Shallow breathing, 61, 137
Short breathing, 137
Siddha Yoga, 26
Skype, 117–18
Sleep, stress and, 119
Smart devices. See Technology
Smith, Will, 147–50
Social activity, 98–99, 116–18

Social media, 117–18
Social norms, 78–79
Somatics, 41–42, 158
Stage fright, 67–68
Stories, personal
    reenacting, 68, 71
    rewriting, 70–71, 74–76, 218
Stress, 93–120
    awareness of, 214
    body movement and, 55–57
    breakdowns from, 101–3
    breathing and, 137
    children and, 115–18
    cultural differences in, 96–99
    detecting, <u>8</u>
    financial, 215
    group exercise for releasing,
        95–96
    from lifestyle, 111–13
    managing, 108–9 (see also
        Rebooting technique [TRT])
    memories triggering, 103–6
    physical response to, 99–101,
        106–8
    physical symptoms and, 158–63
    physiological cycle of, 110–11
    posture and, 118–20, 139–40
    relationships and, 216
    resilience and, 238, 242–43,
        248–57
    technology and, 113–15
    from work, 217
Stress hormones, 108, 136–37
Subconscious thinking
    body movement awareness and,
        57–58
    children, mimicking adults, 76–85
    memories, confusing, 63
    retraining (see Whole Body
        Intelligence [WBI] Lifestyle
        Plan)
    undermining dreams, 238–40
    viral beliefs and, 168, 188, 190
Success, beliefs of, 224
Sufi Order, 27
Support, social, 203–4
Survival instincts, 100
Swami teachers, 26–27
Sweat lodges, 155–56
Sympathetic nervous system, 61,
    133–35, 256–57

T

Technology
  addiction to, 124–25
  distraction of, 14, 246
  posture and, 118–20
  rebooting computers, 128–30
  stress and, 99, 111–15, 121
Tension
  awareness of, 6, 17, 138–39
  in belly, 62
  fear and, 257
  resilience and, 257
  stress and, 102–4, 139–40
Text neck, 118–19
Transcendental Meditation, 133
Trauma, effect of, 147–70
  embedding in body, 152–55
  emotions and cellular memory,
    157–63
  old beliefs and, 150–52
  physical healing and, 163–66
  "poor person" mentality, 147–50
  viral and vital beliefs and, 153–56,
    175–77
Traveling, stress and, 113–15
TRT. *See* Rebooting technique (TRT)

U

Unplugging, step 1 of reboot, 135–37
Urban life, 102–3

V

Video games, 115–18
Violence, stress and, 101–3
Viral beliefs, 171–94
  changing, 187–88, 190, 231
  environmental effect and, 174–75
  limiting self-talk and, 218
  overview, 153–56
  recognizing, 239
  resilience and, 151
  self-assessment for, 168–69
  trauma and, 175–77
  WBI belief process for
    application of, 177–87
    overview, <u>189</u>
    phases of, 190–94

Visualizations
  phase 2 of WBI, 191
  for resilience, 258
  step 6 of reboot, 140–41
  WBI Lifestyle Plan and, 220,
    228
Vital beliefs, 154–55. *See also* Viral
  beliefs
Vogelsong, Ryan "Vogey," 237–38

W

Walking, like parents, 76, 80
War protest, 20–22
Wellness plan, 232
Whole Body Intelligence (WBI)
  affirmations, audio version, 194,
    219, 223
  application of, 39–41, 177–87
  attention, body-first, 3–4
  overview, <u>189</u>
  personal story and creation of,
    19–48
  phases of, 190–94
  resilience and, 250–51
Whole Body Intelligence (WBI)
    Lifestyle Plan, 197–235
  brain adaptability and, 198–200
  format of, 202–3
  practice, importance of, 200–201
  30-day plan, 206–35
  tips for, 203–5
(W)inner Circle, 43
Wisdom, personal, 29
Work performance, 111–13
Work stress, 217
Worry, 127–28. *See also* Stress
Writer's block, 257–58
Writing movement autobiography,
  76–81

Y

Yalapan people, 93–99
Yoga, 24, 26–27